LEWIS&CLARK AND ME

SPENCE CAMPBELL

*To MATT: I really enJoyed
Flying with you.
you ARE A Good piloT
Always Follow your Dreams.
Spence.*

ISBN-13 978-0-9790404-0-5
ISBN-10 0-97904404-0-X

Book designed and printed by
Gorham Printing, Rochester, WA USA

In memory of my late wife Susan,
a wonderful lady,
who saw me through the hard times
and gave me two special sons.

Acknowledgments

Many thanks to the following:

Bill, John and King, who were with me on the swim, Floyd Harvey for his faith and generosity. Gordon Sinclair, and the staff of the Orofino Radio station. All the people and cities that hosted our crew on the swim, My dad for his example of honesty and integrity, My family for their love and concern, My Lewiston high school class of '54 for their support, Mr. Marion Shinn and Mrs. Maude Adams, outstanding teachers who inspired and encouraged me, My High School buddies Charlie and Roy who made my teen years fun, Bill Harris who launched my diving career and E.R. Cross who mentored me throughout it. To Jim Joiner, owner of Best Publishing for his encouragement and technical assistance, Mike Mikowski and Chris Wolf for their editorial suggestions. To Linda Quick and Kelley Sargent for their literary assistance. To my diving buddies Vince Rainier, Mark Schneider, Al Beale and Jerry Gray for their input and support. To Jon Lindbergh for his friendship and kind words and to my wife Marie for her love, patience and help with the book.

Foreword

When I first met Spence Campbell he was working with Dr. Merrill Spencer in the Virginia Mason Research Center diving laboratory in Seattle. The two researchers were evaluating ways to better understand and treat decompression sickness, or in the diver's language "the bends". As a commercial diver with some unhappy experience with that ailment, I was honored and pleased to participate in their program.

Our work in decompression sickness led to the study of using hyperbaric (high pressure) treatments for other medical problems. Spence's ingenuity was to devise simple but effective approaches to diving and hyperbaric procedures. His tenacity in pursuing his goals is illustrated by his single-minded approach to his 557 mile swim described in this book.

As I read Spence's accounts of his boyhood escapades, first flight and commercial diving, I was fascinated by the similarities in our young lives. We both soloed in an Aeronca Champion, we have both felt the shock of a face mask being ripped off by violent water during a commercial dive, we have both acted as guinea pigs during research on very deep dives. I could relate to the humorous and dangerous experiences he describes as they brought back vivid memories of my own youth.

I found this book to be a great story by a man who lived on the raw edges of a tough world: the unforgiving marine environment. The reader, I trust, will agree.

—*Jon M. Lindbergh*

Pioneer Diving Researcher
& Son of Charles Lindbergh

Go West, young man,
and grow up with the country.

HORACE GREELEY

Introduction

I believe it was Horace Greeley who said, "Every young man should have an ordeal" or something like that. Well I guess I had mine.

Writing this book was both fun and cathartic for me. Most of it was written from memory and some notes from a journal I tried to keep when I was on the rivers. Because the swim was done more than forty years ago, lake-like reservoirs have covered the old riverbed and eliminated the series of dangerous rapids referred to in the book.

Thanks to the technical assistance of Mr. Lester Cunningham of the Walla Walla District Corps of Engineers and Mr. Louis Saldamando, Maintenance Supervisor at the U.S. Bureau of Reclamation Hungry Horse dam, I was able to clarify various facts about the rapids on the Snake River and the dives I made in the draft tube tunnels of the Hungry Horse dam.

This was one of the great adventures and challenges in my life and it became my pathway to the future. It is a story that had to be told!

Distance Swimmer

A HERO'S WELCOME greeted Spencer Campbell, marathon swimmer from Orofino, Idaho when he stepped ashore on the banks of the Columbia river at St. Helens Thursday evening.

CHAPTER 1

San Francisco

The fourth day of the Marathon swim had just begun. I was still tired and sore from battling yesterday's 30-mile stretch of storm-tossed Snake River. Today I would have to face two of the most dangerous challenges on the 434 miles left to swim. A few miles down river lay the treacherous Texas and Palouse rapids and just a couple of miles beyond the rapids were the huge whirlpools at Lyons Ferry. Through the years Snake River mariners told intimidating tales about encounters with both of these river monsters. How true those stories were; I was about to find out!

Whatever possessed me to challenge Lewis and Clark to a river race? Could I actually swim the 557 miles of rivers in less than 32 days? Would the rapids, whirlpools, and other dangers prove too much? Did I have the stamina and will to outlast the river?

The stretch of river I was in now was slow moving, peaceful and quiet, like the proverbial calm before the storm. It was around 8:30 and the morning sun was warming up the river canyon. I was swimming on the sunlit side of the river because the warmth felt good on the parts of my body that were above the surface of the water. The current was just strong enough to push me downstream at a good pace so I didn't have to expend much energy. I was just moving along with the current, staring down into the blue-green void. The river's undulating motion and the lack of a visual focus had a mesmerizing effect. After a while my thoughts wandered away to other times and other places. My thoughts raced back over the years.

I could see myself standing alone in a room overlooking a street in San Francisco. Rain was falling against the window, and I was crying!

It was 1939 and I was three years old. My father was awarded custody of me when he and my mother divorced. He wasn't able to take care of me in his one room tenement flat working 10 to 12 hours a day, so I was boarded with a very nice, older widowed woman whom I can only remember as Mrs. Tosh. She was a plump, gentle woman of Swedish descent who spoke softly and smelled of lavender. She read to me at bedtime and fed me oatmeal almost every morning. That's probably why I love lavender scent and don't care much for oatmeal!

I guess the arrangement was that my mother and father would alternate taking me on weekends. My dad never failed to come and get me on his weekend, but I have memories of standing for hours in the upstairs window of the Tosh household on Saturday mornings looking for my mother, crying and stubbornly refusing to leave the window even after being told that she wasn't coming! It happened often enough to still create a potent memory in my mind. Please don't think too harshly of my mother—she was a 33-year-old woman at the time with other problems and two teenage children, my half-brother and sister. Because my mother worked full-time they were semi-loose on the streets of San Francisco.

I really didn't get to know my brother and sister well until I was older. I have some memories of them before my parents divorced. We lived by the railroad tracks in a little house with a white picket fence around it in San Luis Obispo. I think there was a creek running near, or through the backyard, and we lived as a normal, happy family. My sister, Jean, actually named me after an old radio detective program series called, "Spencer Dean and Dan Cassidy."

My dad told me that when I was about one year old, my brother Alan used to take me with him while he sold magazines and newspapers. He would put me in his magazine sack and go door to door on the weekends, selling the *Saturday Evening Post*. In the evenings, he would put me in his newspaper sack; go out on a busy street corner. He would holler "Paaaper" and I would try to imitate him with my tiny voice "paa-pa." Dad said it was freezing cold and I would have a stocking cap pulled over my head. Only my eyes and my little, cold, red nose would be visible peeking over the top of the sack. He said I sold a lot of papers for Alan.

I remember my sister and my brother fighting like brothers and sisters do. Alan loved to tease Jean, and she hated it. They both seemed to love me. We had a cat named Rusty and a little terrier dog whose name I can't remember. After my parents divorced, I lost track of my brother and sister until later in my life.

After living with Mrs. Tosh until I was four years old my father moved me to a new boarding home. It was just across the street from the Tosh home, and I moved in with a family named Brennigan. They had a son my age named George. Mr. Brennigan was a tall, thin, stern looking Scotsman with a heavy brogue. I don't remember much about Mrs. Brennigan—maybe because Mr. Brennigan was such a strong figure. The house was immaculate and Mrs. Brennigan was a fastidious housekeeper. She prepared good food and introduced me to Popeye's favorite. Oddly, to this day I love spinach with mayonnaise on it as she used to serve the family.

The Brennigans were sophisticated people with a heavy emphasis on literature and the arts. Mr. Brennigan read Shakespeare to us and taught us to recite the "To be or not to be" soliloquy. Even though neither George, nor I knew what it meant we would puff up and strut around the house asking, "whether it was nobler for the mind to suffer the slings and arrows of outrageous fortunes."

At age five I was enrolled with George in a private dramatics class. Our teacher's name was Mrs. Wilson, whom my father later told me had personally trained several famous actors and actresses. I don't remember who he said they were. Anyway, I seemed to have a real flair for dramatics and poor George did not. I excelled at it enough to perform on the Major Boles amateur hour at age five. I recited a dramatic poem and sang "God Bless America." Poor George had a bad case of stage fright and muffed a couple of performances, so the Brennigans lost interest in George's acting career and dropped the lessons!

That was the end of my acting career, too, until high school where I performed in all the high school plays and some civic theater productions. I later found out that my father's support for my theatrics was due to his secret desire to become an actor himself. He kind of lived vicariously through my amateur acting venues. I lived with the Brennigans until I was seven and they took good care of me. God bless them wherever they are now. I hope George got over his fear of speaking in public. With parents like the Brennigans, he must have grown-up to be a well-educated, principled man.

I was seven when my father remarried. He took me to live with him and my new stepmother in Richmond, across the Bay from San Francisco. My dad was a machinist foreman in the Kaiser shipyards. He met my stepmother there. She was a welder and was working on the same ship as my dad. These were the war years—times were difficult and certain foods were rationed.

I only have four vivid memories of that time in Richmond. One was when I got a bad cold and my dad, who was a great master of old home remedies, put a "mustard plaster" on my chest. This is a concoction of mustard and I'm not sure what else! It stunk to high heaven, and I don't know if it worked to cure my cold, but I sure felt a lot better when I got rid of it! I was also treated to several teaspoons of sugar and coal oil. My stepmother was 20 years old and came off of a farm in northern Idaho. She too had many homespun remedies. When I was about 10 and in grade school I remember wearing a bag of herbs around my neck to ward off colds!

The second memory of Richmond was my dad teaching me how to box. He had been a Prize Fighter in his twenties and had fought what they called "curtain risers" for headline fights in the San Francisco area. He had been pretty good, but considered it too tough a profession. I guess I kind of took to it naturally. He bought two large pair of boxing gloves, and I had a lesson nearly every night for a year. When I was eight years old, he enrolled me in a junior boxing program at the neighborhood Jewish Community Center. Although we were not Jewish, they accepted children of other faiths into their program. I trained there for a couple of months and had several matches. I won all of them and the center wanted to put me on their junior team. I don't remember why I didn't go any further with my boxing, but I didn't.

I do remember that a Mexican kid about my age who lived a block or so from us kept bullying me and threatening to beat me up. My dad arranged a front-yard boxing match between us. We put on the gloves and I beat him all over the yard for about two minutes before he threw off the gloves and ran home crying! The word got out and I wasn't bothered much by bullies after that.

The next recollection I have was when my dad decided I was old enough to go to the store and get some eggs, milk, and meat—all of which were rationed. He gave me some money and some ration stamps. When I returned from the store with the meat, milk and eggs, I gave my dad his money back. He looked at it and said, "Didn't you pay for the food?" I said that I gave them the stamps and that they didn't take any money! My dad took me back to the store and paid them for the food. They had no idea how I'd gotten away with just giving them the stamps. I didn't think to give them money because no one asked me for any money! It was sort of like a *Leave it to Beaver* episode. Even though it was an innocent kid mistake my father was a principled man and believed in doing the right thing.

The last clear memory of Richmond is when my stepmother came home crying that my dad was seriously hurt and in the hospital. I remember being scared that my dad would die and I would be boarded out again! My dad was seriously injured when a high-pressure air hose burst and started whipping all over the machine shop. My dad was trying to get his workers out of the shop when the large high-pressure hose hit him above the hips in the back, lifted him 3 feet in the air and threw him about 15 feet across the shop, down a hallway, and onto a concrete floor. He came home from the hospital all banged up in a back brace. It was about two months before he could stand and walk, and three months later that he was able to return to work.

One last thing about Richmond was that my dad was able to get my brother, Allan, a job at the shipyard and Allan came to visit me several times while he was working with my dad. I really liked my big brother! He raced motorcycles at the Belmar track in San Francisco and did other cool things.

My dad was somewhat of a dreamer, and he and my stepmother, Jean, decided that they wanted to leave California and take an adventure—a car trip to Port Arthur, Canada to visit my dad's mother—a grandmother I had never met. After the Canada visit they planned to go back to Idaho to start a new life.

My dad bought a Model A Ford with a rumble seat. He and my uncle, Ray Moe who was a carpenter, removed the rumble seat and built a wooden pickup bed extension. They fashioned a canvas top for the pickup bed and we ended up with a 1945 mechanized Ford Conestoga wagon! It was a unique modification that drew all sorts of looks and comments, but it was functional.

The war ended in August 1945 and my dad spent the remainder of the year and the next spring preparing for the exodus from Richmond. In late May of 1946, the Campbells loaded up their wagon and headed north to Canada. By this time I had a baby brother who was about one year old. The trip to Canada turned out to be a real adventure. We camped out a lot on the trip and we fished and did some sightseeing along the way. I remember it was a long way to Canada. I rode most of the way in the back of the modified Conestoga Pickup.

The main thing I remember about the trip was camping somewhere in Oregon and visiting some of my stepmother's relatives. Their kids and I played a lot in the forest down by a creek. I got into poison oak and got it all over my face and upper body. As sung in the 1950's song, Poison Ivy, "It took an ocean of calamine lotion!" I was painted from head to waist with the pink liquid that dried into a hard paste and felt terrible! Of course I scratched the itching areas and some of it became infected. The trip from Oregon to Michigan was a pink nightmare! I finally got over it, although I wore the scares from my bout with poison oak until we retuned from Canada to Idaho.

The one major incident on the trip happened somewhere in the middle of Montana. My dad put his jacket on top of the cab of the truck and drove off. After about 15 miles he missed the jacket and remembered that he had put it on top of the cab—it was gone! In the jacket pocket was his billfold with a few thousand dollars in it—all the money we had in the world!

As fast as the little Ford would go we retreated the 15 miles we had just driven. We passed about eight cars coming our way, but needless to say, no one passed us going our way! When we got near the place where we had stopped my dad saw his jacket about 200 yards down the highway on the side of the road. The billfold was still in his jacket with all the money. God was watching over the Campbells that day!

My grandmother lived in a big Tudor house on the shores of Lake Superior. Everyone in the Canadian family spoke French and I had no idea what they were saying. I didn't know that my dad could speak fluent French until he joined in the family reunion stories. After four days he was communicating like a native. Even though my dad's family all spoke English, they preferred to speak French, except when they spoke to my stepmother and me. My grandmother was a kind, jolly, gray-haired woman. She was of substantial build and reminded me somewhat of Mrs. Tosh, because she also smelled of lavender. Between my Grandmother and two of my aunts they cooked some fantastic food. At times I wasn't sure what I was eating, but it all tasted so good I didn't really care!

After a couple of weeks we left Port Arthur and started our trip to Idaho. We did some sight seeing as we went through Glacier National Park. I don't remember much of the trip, except that I thought North Dakota was end-to-end wheat fields. After that trip every time I heard the phrase, "amber waves of grain," I thought they must mean North Dakota. Eventually, we arrived in Princeton, Idaho—a very small town with a population of about 250 souls.

Princeton Idaho is located about 60 miles southeast of Spokane, Washington in Idaho farm and timber country. About eighty percent, or more of the residents of Princeton, were either farmers or lumberjacks. This was the location of the farm of my stepmother's parents—the Mayberry's—fancy that! We would stay at the farm with them for the rest of the summer and fall of 1946.

CHAPTER 2

The Ranch

We must have drifted over to a shallow part of the river because my thoughts of the ranch were interrupted by the sight of a large section of sharp, jagged corrugated tin roofing a couple feet below me in the dark river water. In a second I was fully alert and got my faculties together just in time to swim to the side of several large rolls of old barbed wire which were stacked up on the shallow bottom and came to within a few inches of the surface—a dangerous snag for a power boat or a swimmer! I suggested to the support crew that we move further offshore, and they turned our boat the *No-Name* toward the middle of the river. Moments later I was staring into empty, deep water again and before long my thoughts returned to the ranch in Princeton.

We arrived at the ranch in midsummer, between spring planting, but before the fall harvest. My grandparents had a small farm, with two large pastures, a huge wheat field and some timberland. They had three horses, two workhorses, and a saddle horse named Brownie that was too wild to ride. They also had several cows and a really mean bull! Even though it looked like a farm to me, the Mayberry's preferred to call their farm a ranch.

This was a lull period between the intense ranch work seasons and my grandparents had some free time to spend playing host and getting to know my dad and me. My new grandpa used to be a horse wrangler. He wrangled wild horses from the Badlands near Terry, Montana. He toured the rodeo circuits, drove cattle, and did most every job that horsemen can do. He was an expert on horses.

Up until this time I had lived all my life in a large city. I thought eggs were manufactured and came in cardboard cartons. Even though I liked to play cowboy, I had no clue what ranch life was like, or what real cowboys did. My new grandparents gave us a tour of the farm. They told me about the animals and said they would teach me to ride the horses. I was warned about the mean bull and the electric fences. The month of June went by quickly, and on the Fourth of July they had a large patriotic celebration in Princeton. This Fourth of July had special meaning since it was the first one following the war years.

The rest of July was filled with exploring the ranch and I learned to ride the big workhorse, Charlie. They taught me how to shoot the 22 caliber rifle and I learned about ranch chores.

By August 15, I had almost completed Ranching 101. I was getting to know a lot of the kids from nearby farms, and because we still had some summer playtime left before the fall harvest season began, several of the kids came over to our ranch and we would swing from the barn loft and drop into a big pile of hay. We went swimming in the Potlatch Creek swimming hole and did a bunch of other things. The kids were fun, but merciless! Since I was the city kid, I was the butt of every farm kid prank that could be played!

One night about five of the boys talked me into going snipe hunting. I remember holding the burlap bag open on a small game trail about a mile out in the woods waiting for the wily snipe that my friends said was very rare and had never been captured. They said if I got one I would be the first local kid hero for catching a snipe! About 11 p.m. I got real cold. The full moon cast spooky shadows on the ground through the trees and I heard weird noises coming from the woods. I got scared, and turned on the flashlight I had borrowed from my grandfather's garage. I went over to another trail where I thought I would find my friend, Ben, guarding his snipe bag. He was gone! (Actually, home to bed.) The weird noises seemed to grow louder, and one of them sounded like a growl! So much for "snipe hunting." I covered three quarters of a mile to the ranch house in world record time!

There's no panic like that conjured up in a kid's mind if they think that something weird is chasing them! Forget that I was only 4'4" tall. Three strand barbwire fences single bound! Broad jump a 10 foot creek, no problem! When I got to the ranch house my grandparents were worried sick that I had gotten lost and they were about to start a search for me.

When they heard about the snipe hunt and how a big snipe growled at me, they all laughed and laughed. I didn't see anything funny to laugh at until my Uncle Winford sat me down and explained about all the pranks that the kids would try to play on me. Then the thought of me out there alone lying for three hours on a game trail a mile in the woods with an open burlap bag excitedly waiting to be the first kid to ever catch a non-existent snipe made me laugh too!

My Uncle Winn was a great guy, "drop-dead" good-looking, with features like a movie star. He was in great shape, and because he was raised on the ranch, he knew about everything you can do on a ranch. He not only warned me about all the standard tricks the kids would try to pull, but he helped me pull a couple of new ones on them! Like his dad, he was a great horseman and use to do some rodeo work (pickup-man), I believe. He was great with horses and he taught me to ride. He was always trying to ride our wild saddle horse, Brownie.

My grandpa acquired the horse when Winn was away in the Navy. Winn tried everything to tame Brownie but the horse was too wild, unpredictable, and dangerous and Winn finally gave up on him and told his dad to sell the horse to someone who had a string of rodeo bucking horses. Several years later Brownie had become quite well-known for being one of the hot, wild "saddle broncs" in the rodeo circuit. When I was in my last year of grade school someone told the family that Brownie had broken his neck jumping out of a moving horse trailer. He was wild to the very end!

In mid August, we started harvest on the ranch, bailing hay, chocking wheat, and a lot of hard, hot, dusty work from dawn till dusk. I soon learned that you earned your keep if you lived on a ranch. By school time I started getting used to ranch life. Because of my love for riding the old workhorse, Charlie, and my interest in taking care of him, my grandpa took a shine to me.

In later years when I worked on the ranch during summer vacation, he taught me how to hook up a team of workhorses and use them to skid logs out of the woods after they had been limbed and peeled. In addition to ranching, Grandpa and Uncle Winn supplemented their ranching income by logging and making telephone poles. By the time I was eleven I could limb and peel poles, and by twelve, I could drive the skidding team.

Although it was interesting to learn about the woods and horses, it was hard work and very dangerous, and I didn't care for it much.

At harvest time we used the old John Deere tractor. It was a big green and yellow machine with two huge rear tires, with bar-like treads and it had two small, and angled front wheels. You started it by pulling over a huge flywheel. It would go "chug-chug". Finally, if you pulled it hard enough to make the cylinders fire, it would start; then you could drive it anywhere!

At first, I wasn't strong enough to spin the flywheel so I got the job of shutting the engine off when we were finished with the tractor. To shut it off you pulled the magneto wire out of its holder and the machine would quit. The magneto wire was a short loop of heavy gauge wire with a metal connector on one end; you just pulled it out of the magneto-housing socket to kill the tractor engine. The main problem was that the small loop of wire was so short that your finger would accidentally touch the metal connector before the engine came to a complete stop and the magneto would deliver you a stout electrical shock! It seemed like I would always touch the metal when I shut off the engine. Whenever I jumped from the shock my Grandpa would chuckle. I didn't much like being the shut off man. In the ensuing years when I worked on the farm in the summer I would be able to start and drive the old John Deere tractor and do all the tractor work that was necessary. I actually got pretty good at it.

One of my other chores at the ranch was to get the mail. The mailbox was about a half mile from house by road, but less than one quarter of a mile if you cut diagonally across the pasture. There was only one problem with that. It was the domain of the bull. One day while I was going to get the mail, I sneaked across the pasture trying not to draw the attention of the bull; the mean bull, the really mean bull! But three quarters of the way across he spotted me and the race was on! I barely made it to the fence before he got to me. From then on I took the long way to the mailbox!

Another one of my jobs on the ranch was to ride the horse over to the neighbor's farm every week to get milk, because we had no dairy cows. The people were very nice and had a pretty young daughter about my age. They also had a huge Tom Turkey that strutted around the yard and acted very hostile to me. Every time I got off the horse, he chased me. I had to run to the porch of the house to escape him! He intimidated me to the point that I didn't want to go get the milk. I told my dad that I was afraid of the turkey. My dad laughed and said it was just a turkey, and not to be afraid of it because I was bigger. He said if it threatened me, I should fight it and teach it a lesson so it wouldn't bother me anymore.

Bolstered by my dad's encouragement, the next time I went to get the milk I stepped off the horse confidently, resolved to protect myself and do battle with the turkey if necessary. The turkey was in the yard. As usual he spotted me immediately, came on full speed, and the battle was on! The turkey was a lot stronger than I expected; he flew at me and grabbed the front of my shirt with his talons. I punched him, and he scratched and flogged me. The battle only lasted a few minutes before I realized I was losing, so I grabbed him around his skinny neck and squeezed with all my might. It must have shut off all his air, because in a few minutes he went limp. I kept choking him for a few more seconds and then pushed him away, got up, and kicked him! He sailed about 6 feet in the air before landing in a pile. I watched him for a few minutes, but he didn't move.

I went to the door of the farmhouse, rang the bell, and asked for my milk. I told them that the turkey had attacked me and that I beat him up! I got my milk, mounted my horse, and went home. I was pleased with myself and could hardly wait to tell my dad about my conquest over the turkey! When I went to get milk the next week, the turkey saw me coming and ran off. I didn't mind going to get the milk after that.

School started in September; the schoolhouse was in Princeton, about four miles from the ranch. Surprise! My school bus was "Charlie." I rode him back and forth to school for about three months. The school was very small in an old converted two-story house. There were six elementary grades. I remember there were three grades on the bottom floor in one-room and all the older grades were on the top floor. There were only about five kids in my grade, but more in the older grades. I don't know how the teachers handled it, but it must have been interesting! Schools at that time were big on penmanship, English, history, and geography. Next came math and science. There were few problem students, except for those with learning disabilities. Respect for your elders and people in authority was ingrained in our behavior and you could get in as much trouble from your fellow students as you could with the teachers and parents if you acted up in school.

Winter fell on Princeton, Idaho, and I had a week or two of riding the horse to school in the snow. It was cold and not much fun, especially when it was wet, slushy snow. I remember I had a pair of old worn-out wool mittens and my hands would freeze holding the reins. About a week before Thanksgiving my father announced that he had formed a partnership in a house painting business in Lewiston and that we would be moving in a few days.

Lewiston, Idaho was a small town with a population of about 19,000 people, but according to the Mayberry's, we were moving to the big city. I kind of loved the ranch by now, but with the winter weather, it was kind of boring except for the sled riding. I wasn't really looking forward to riding the horse to school anymore in deep, freezing snow! I silently thanked God for his excellent timing. Again, we loaded our belongings in our "Conestoga" Ford wagon and set out for Lewiston.

CHAPTER 3

My Dad

It was either a very large fish, or my eyes playing tricks, but about 12 to 14 feet below me I saw a huge shadow. It appeared to be about six feet long, and it was moving upstream with a snake-like motion. It was too deep in the murky water for me to actually see what it was, but it gave me an uncomfortable feeling, like when you are a kid swimming in deep, dark water. You might imagine that there is some horrible underwater monster trying to grab your legs.

When I was a kid, I set several world records swimming from the deep water in the Lewiston millpond to the safety of the log boom walkway, where you could quickly pull yourself out of the water just before the monster grabbed your leg! Now being an adult, and a commercial deep-sea diver, I wasn't frightened by the imaginary water monsters of childhood, but there can still be a subtle fear of the unknown in anyone. For the next quarter-mile I kept looking for the shadow. I never saw it again. We had a few miles to go before we would reach the Texas Rapids, and the river was still slow and restful. Soon, I drifted off again. I thought about my dad and how this crazy river stunt got started.

Sixteen years had passed since my child hood experiences on the ranch and the start of the swim. Though the time between these events was relatively short, it was packed with a lifetime of memories. It was mid May of 1961 when I moved my wife Susan and my one year old son, Ron, from Spokane, Washington to Orofino, Idaho, a small logging town nestled between brown rolling hills on the Clearwater river. Orofino was 44 miles east of Lewiston up the river. Lewiston was my hometown, and since I had spent countless hours exploring all the nearby towns and hunting areas as a kid, I felt as if it was a kind of return to my roots.

We had come to Orofino for two reasons. My father had a crippling case of pulmonary emphysema. Years of heavy smoking and spraying lead based paints had severely damaged his lungs. I felt as if we might be of some help if we lived closer. The second reason was that the diving work had run out, and my employer Bill Harris Divers of Spokane was between diving contracts. I needed work to support my family and I figured I could find some temporary work in Orofino and be close to my father too.

I thought a lot about my dad as I drove from Spokane to Orofino. To me my dad was always strong and invincible. He was easy to talk to about anything and I recalled some memories of his guidance through my teens.

When I was a sophomore in high school I had met some kids from downtown Lewiston who were a little wild and inclined to get into trouble. They were always in fights and ran around late at night with three or four other kids with the same tendencies. They had found a way to get into a large grain elevator in Lewiston and would go in at night and play around. They said you could jump off the walkways into the wheat piles and that it was a lot of fun. Several of them had moms, but no dads, and they seemed to be able to get away with staying out late at night. I had a curfew, unless I asked my dad to stay out later. I told my Dad that the guys wanted me to go out to the grain elevator with them that night.

My dad was a painting contractor and knew lots of people in town. He had several friends on the Lewiston police force and he knew about the reputation of these kids.

He was also a homespun philosopher and a natural psychologist. I never remember him telling me I couldn't do something. He would just talk me through the thinking process and bring me face-to-face with the facts. Then he would allow me to make my own decisions. It would go something like this: (Dad) "Who are these kids?" (Me): "Just some kids from school." (Dad) "Is it their grain elevator?" (Me) "No." (Dad) "Do they have permission to go into the grain elevator?" (Me) "I don't think so." (Dad) "How do they get into the grain elevator?" (Me) "They know a way to get in." (Dad) "Do you think people that own the grain elevator want these kids to go in there?" (Me). "Probably not." (Dad.) "If the cops found them in there, do you think they would get into trouble?" (Me) "I guess so." (Dad) "How would you feel if the cops caught you in the elevator with them and took you to the station and called me?" (Me) "I wouldn't want that to happen."

By this time, the cold logic of getting into serious trouble killed my enthusiasm I made up my mind that I didn't want to go anymore! He never said no, he just convinced me to make the right decisions. He always used the psychology of telling me I was too smart to get into serious trouble. He always praised my common sense to make the right decisions and it worked. Later I would use the same approach with my two sons when they were in high school and there were drugs and other serious traps for them to fall into. It worked for them too!

I was not much of a high school athlete, except for the judo team and the gymnastic team. I was on the high school archery team and acted in all the high school plays. My high school grades were mediocre, except for choir and English. I loved science, but I had a bad start with mathematics.

During my senior year I took an elective course in descriptive science. My teacher was Mr. Marion Shinn, who taught chemistry in our school. He was an ex-submarine sailor and a tremendous teacher. He took a special interest in me and lit a fire in me for science that never went out!

I tied the school record for the number of points you could get in that class, and as a result of Mr. Shinn's mentoring and encouragement, I took a half a semester of unaccredited chemistry and did OK. Little did I know at that time that the special motivation and confidence that he gave me would inspire me to accomplish breakthrough research in the field of submarine medicine later in my life.

I took a class in high school called "family living." It was a sort of a predecessor to some of the social classes taught in high school and colleges today. One evening my dad asked me what we were studying in family living and I told him we were studying security and welfare. He asked me what I thought security was? I told him that I thought it was having a nice big home, new cars and lots of money in the bank. He thought for a minute and said, "Well, that's what some people think it is." I was curious, and said, "Dad, what do you think, security is?" Without hesitation my Dad looked at me and said, "Son, real security is being able to walk into the deep woods bare-butt naked, and walk out again a year later." I think what he was trying to tell me was that personal security and welfare was a function of personal skill, personal responsibility, and a will to survive.

One time, Dad was trying to give me some advice about being cautious when making serious changes in life. He asked me if I had heard the saying "The grass always looks greener on the other side of the fence." I said that I had, and he said, "Think about it this way. The reason the grass is greener in the other pasture, is that it's longer and uncut. In your pasture the livestock have eaten it short, and exposed all the piles of horse and cow manure. One advantage to staying in your own pasture is that you're not likely to step in something you can't see!" Having had some of those pasture-switching decisions in my life, I now know what he meant!

Another time, we were talking about taxes. My dad always said that he did not resent paying his fair share of taxes, but that taxes should have limits. "But we need taxes from people to do all the neat stuff our government does for us," I said. My Dad took 20 pennies from our penny jar and laid them on the table in front of me. "Pretend this is all the money you earn. I come to you and say we're building a great road that we all need and it's a real good thing. You can help by giving two cents. Now, that's not much. Look at all the pennies you have." I agreed and he took two cents. Then he said that the government needed two cents more for another very worthy cause and I contributed two more cents. He continued with worthy cause after worthy cause until my 20 pennies were gone. Then I understood why we needed limits on taxes.

My Dad was an avid fisherman, and he liked to fish for steelhead in the Clearwater River. He was a good fisherman and caught lots of steelhead. He would sit out in a small wooden rowboat for hours and hours in the river just to catch one fish. I didn't see how he had the patience. He would always offer to take me with him, but I was a little too hyper to be able to tolerate three to four hours of fishing. He did take me to Soldier's Meadow for some camping and lake fishing in the summer and I liked that because I could fish for a while and then go do something else if I wanted.

One early morning about 5 a.m., the Fish and Game Department came to the lake with their fish transfer truck and dumped hundreds of rainbow trout into the lake. I was one of the only people up at that time so I offered to help the fish and game officer while he made the transfer. Some of the trout had been injured on the trip from the hatchery and didn't make it. There were about 25 rainbow trout, 9-12 inches long, that were floating on the surface after the dump. The fish and game officer said they were still good fish; they just didn't make the trip or the transfer. He said I could have all of them I could net off the surface and he gave me a little sticker to authorize possession of the fish. He then loaded up his stuff and left.

I was excited! I waded into the lake and got about three or four nice trout, and ran back to our camp to show my dad who was just getting up. He said to take our small boat out and net as many as I could. He would come and clean them and pack them in our ice chest. By 7 a.m. I had salvaged most of the fish, and my dad was down by the lake cleaning trout and packing them away. Campers and fisherman were starting their morning routines and some of them had seen me out netting the dead fish. Several people had gathered around my dad where he was cleaning the fish. By then, I had netted the last fish I could find and joined my dad on the bank. My Dad explained to the onlookers that the fish department had authorized us to salvage the fish, and he graciously offered to share some of the 30 plus trout we had salvaged with anyone who was willing to clean them.

One of the onlookers was a painting contractor from our town, a competitor of my Dad's who lived in a nice big house on a hill above town; he didn't like my dad or his partner. He was a big heavyset man with jowls, and he stood watching my dad cleaning the trout. As a deliberate put down he said in a loud voice, "You're not going to eat those dead fish, are you, Harry?" My Dad slowly turned his head from his fish cleaning and looked up at his heckling competitor and said, "Well, (name), I don't usually eat live ones." The small crowd broke out laughing and the man huffed and walked off. I was proud of my Dad and the dead fish tasted great too!

My Dad finally bought a house on Main Street about one half block and diagonally across the street from Campbell's Corner. It was an older style house with a large front porch and a big backyard. By this time I had two new sisters, Gerry and Jackie. The side of our house bordered a tavern on the corner where Main Street turned left to the stockyards. There was a pretty tall fence and a wide driveway between the tavern and the house. The music and the loud talk from the tavern didn't bother us much. There wasn't much of a criminal element in the area either. The greatest fear our parents had was that we might get run over, or fall off of something.

On the other side of our house was a huge vacant lot, which lay between our house and Auntie Miller's court where we used to live. It was great to finally have a house. What I liked most about it was the many lilac bushes that surrounded our house. They smelled so great when they were in bloom in spring. Another thing I liked about the house was that it had a small two-room cottage in our backyard. This became my bedroom, and my makeshift science laboratory. I spent many memorable moments in that little house.

I had several chemistry sets given to me over the years for Christmas presents and a small telescope. I was mostly fascinated by astronomy. When I was about 12, I had a job delivering Collier's magazine. It was one of the first magazines to run a series of articles and artists renderings of space travel and stories about man going to the moon. The magazine featured articles by the German scientist, Werner Von Braun. They had great colored pictures and conceptual artwork. I cut out the pictures from the articles and pasted them up in my makeshift laboratory.

I got very interested in making rockets, and with the help of my friend, Buddy Randall, built a big rocket out of a thick cardboard mailing tube. We concocted our own brand of rocket fuel and packed it into our rocket engine cavity. We attached a set of fins and fashioned a nose cone that actually had a parachute in it. We painted it silver and black. When it was finished, the rocket stood about 4 feet high and looked like a real rocket should. We decided to launch it at the airport late at night. Generally, no one was there much after dark. We reckoned that if it exploded, no one would hear it, and if it caught fire, we could put it out before anyone came.

About 10:30 one night, Buddy and I and a friend of ours took the rocket up to Hillcrest Airport. This friend shall remain nameless to protect the young and foolish. It was a dark, starless night and the airport was deserted. We took the big rocket out to the middle of the field and set it up for the launch. We lit the dynamite fuse that went up into the fuel and ran to our protected observation point. The dynamite fuse sputtered with its faint flame and after a moment it burned its way up into the rocket engine nozzle. We held our breaths, but nothing happened!

We waited for about 30 seconds more. Still nothing! It was then that our friend, who had a penchant for stupid stunts, got up and ran toward the rocket assuming that the fuse had gone out. It hadn't! Buddy and I were yelling at him to stay away, but he got within five feet of the rocket as the ignition sequence timed itself perfectly to catch our friend (soon to be rocket fodder) within four feet of blastoff! It was a spectacular ignition that lit up an area of about 20 feet with the initial burn and we could see the figure of our friend silhouetted against the light of the takeoff flare. We watched in amazement as the big rocket lifted slowly off the asphalt and rose to a height of about 25 feet. It was a spectacular site for us, but not nearly as spectacular as it must have been for our friend who almost got aboard before the launch!

He was directly below the blast site frozen, looking up at the rocket climbing above him. Then it happened! The heat from the burning rocket fuel burned through the cardboard tube and the upward thrust became sideward thrust on all sides. The rocket slowed its' upward climb and hovered for a moment about 40 feet above the ground while it spewed out an umbrella-like pattern of fire and sparks. Unfortunately, our foolish friend was under that umbrella, and for a moment, he was totally obscured by the fireworks.

Then the rocket pitched over on its side and headed back toward earth on a descending, diagonal path away from our friend who was still smoldering under the takeoff path! The flaming rocket hit the ground about 70 feet away from our friend and exploded into a big ball of fire and sparks.

When the fireworks died down, Buddy and I got up and ran over to our friend who had not appeared to move a muscle since ignition. It was a cold fall night and he was wearing a heavy, black wool overcoat and a wide brimmed black hat. When we approached, him we could see the live cinders glowing in many places in his overcoat. His hat was actually on fire with a small flame! Smoke was flowing from all the little burned holes in his coat and hat. He just stood there in shock, looking in the direction of the crashed rocket. He didn't seem to be hurt; he just seemed to be on fire!

The picture of him standing there, smoldering in the aftermath, was too much for Buddy and me and we broke into hysterical laughter as our friend finally moved and slowly removed his burning hat! When he saw the flame, he threw his hat on the ground and stomped out the fire. Buddy and I howled! After we helped him put out his burning clothes, we cleaned up our rocket crash site and left for home.

I know that my Dad would have had words for me if he knew about the explosive nature of the rocket. I don't think he ever found out, and so far as I know, no one but we three boys ever witnessed Lewiston, Idaho's first failed space shot!!

It was hard to picture my Dad in his present condition. He was hardly able to walk from one room in the house to another without the aid of his oxygen tank. In spite of his infirmity, he always seemed to be in good spirits, and he still managed an occasional trip to the Asahka tavern to swap stories with his friends. "Hair of the dog" he used to claim with a weak smile as he would drink a beer or a small glass of whiskey and take a few puffs on a favorite cigar.

CHAPTER 4

Orofino

My father and stepmother had moved from Lewiston to Orofino and now lived on a small acreage about six miles south of Orofino. My folks property was on a corner of the Cavendish grade, overlooking beautiful timbered hillsides that sloped down to the Clearwater River. Just a few miles down the grade was the small one tavern, one store town of Asahka. A couple of miles northwest of Asahka was "Bruce's Eddy", then a famous local landmark on the North Fork of the Clearwater River, and now the site of Idaho's Dwarshak Dam. Almost directly across the main Clearwater River from Asahka was another famous landmark known as Canoe Campsite. It was the staging and starting place for the famous Lewis and Clark expedition down the Clearwater, Snake and Columbia Rivers to the Pacific Ocean.

At that time all my younger brothers and sisters were still at home. My brother, Bill, from the "Conestoga Model A Ford" days, was a senior in high school. My sister, Gerri, was a couple of years behind him, and the rest of the Campbell kids, Jackie, Sheila, Mike, and Mona were all about two years apart in age.

Susan and I rented a small apartment at one end of Main Street in the small town of Orofino. Our apartment sat on the edge of a steep hill at the end of Main Street and looked out over the town. For some reason it was called Canada Hill. We had a million-dollar view of the surrounding timber covered hills and the beautiful Clearwater River.

Susan was now pregnant with our second child, Scott. Diving work was scarce for Bill Harris and I took a job at the state psychiatric hospital located on the outskirts of town. Ever since I was in high school I had a love for science and the biological and medical areas were most intriguing to me. The state hospital was advertising for people to train as Psychiatric Aides. I thought the training might be challenging and interesting, and I needed a job!

I qualified for the training at the hospital and started class the next week. We were given an abbreviated version of Psychology 100, some Abnormal Psychology, and then moved onto symptoms and manifestations of various types of psychosis, neurosis, and other mental problems. We were trained to measure and dispense medications and give shots. I found the training to be fascinating and very thorough. After training there were several areas of the hospital that needed aides. Because I had received the highest scores in the medical and psychological tests, I was assigned to the hospital ward. In the hospital ward I worked under a wonderful head nurse, Mrs. Allen. We seem to hit it off right away. She continued to teach me about nursing and medical procedures. There was a shortage of qualified doctors and nurses for this field of medicine at the state hospital. Aides were trained to assist in a multitude of medical procedures, including x-ray and minor surgical operations.

After six months, I felt more like medical intern than a Psychiatric Aide. The hospital work ignited my interest in biological science and I used the resources of the hospital and public library to read everything I could about the medical sciences. I even saved a few dollars from the little salary I earned to buy the "College Outline

Series" paperback books on Biology, Anatomy, Physiology, Anthropology, and Psychology.

After I had been at the hospital for a few months they acquired a new Laboratory Manager. He had a Ph.D. in medical technology and had spent about 12 years in intensive research. He just wanted to take a timeout in a small town and do routine medical tests for a while. The hospital was delighted to get such a talented person, even if it wasn't a permanent situation. The manager, who I will call Bob, needed a lab technician. I applied for the position and got it.

I transferred to the lab for about four months and performed on-the-job training under Bob. He was a brilliant man who really knew his stuff, and he taught me a lot in the brief time that I worked with him. Unfortunately, the hospital acquired a Certified Lab Technician and I was reassigned where the hospital needed me the most.

My new assignment was on the men's receiving ward. This is where all the new male patients were sent after they were admitted until the medical staff could assess their psychological conditions, and in many cases, get them under medical control. All types of mental patients came to us and there were some who posed a physical threat to the staff and other patients. There were always two male attendants on the men's receiving ward and we were all trained in physical restraint techniques.

The receiving ward consisted of an open bay of single beds leading from the ward office to a large heavy, locked door through which there was a hall and a stairway out of the building. On the other side of the ward office was a large day room with a television and game tables for those patients who could participate.

Beyond the day room were showers, bathrooms, and a long hallway with locked rooms on either side for the more difficult patients. After you exited the ward through the heavy door into the hall and the stairway there were two other locked doors that you had to pass through to get outside the building. It was a pretty secure facility.

The education and experience I got in the six months spent on that word was both fascinating and depressing. Several months after I was assigned to the receiving ward I completed some additional training and was awarded a Psychiatric Aide II rating. I was given the job of Night Shift Supervisor of the men's receiving ward. My shift was from 4 p.m. to midnight. I liked that shift because after all the patients were in bed it gave me time to study academic subjects between medications and security rounds.

Our office was situated in the middle of the ward so we could observe all the hallways and the dayroom activities. The ward office was screened with heavy chain-link wire and had a Dutch door through which we dispensed medications. The office was secure and kept locked unless occupied by the attendants. During the night shift the staff remained in the office after lights out unless administering to a patient or making rounds.

CHAPTER 5

Desperation and Challenge

radually I became aware of the unmistakable sound of fast moving water, then I heard the underwater sound of a disturbed river bottom. I raised my head quickly and looked down river expecting to see the start of the Texas rapids. My brother, Bill, must have noticed me looking downstream and he called to me, "Spence, it's not the big one yet. It looks like about 50 or 60 yards of fast shallow channel. The river smooths out again after that."

The small shallow channel with its mild rapids was easy to navigate, and I only scraped against a couple of big rocks as I passed through into the smooth water beyond. So far my training and conditioning had paid off. I could only hope it would get me through the most dangerous part of the river coming up in a few miles. For now the river was still, quiet and restful and before long I returned to my thoughts of how I came to be here doing this swim.

It was really an act of desperation initiated by circumstances. The state hospital job was interesting, but unfulfilling. As the early spring of 1962 melted the snows of the northern Idaho winter, I became very restless and dissatisfied with my life as it was. I felt driven to set and accomplish some major goals to be successful. I wanted to do something to work toward that goal, rather than waiting for circumstances to shape my future. I really wanted to do something in medicine, but I had no formal college and I still had a deep desire to stay in the diving field.

Through the last weeks of March, and the first weeks of April, I was plagued with feelings of acute anxiety and frustration. My attitude started to deteriorate and I seemed to have lost interest in almost everything. Our financial situation was grim; I described it as "broke and owing." I felt like I was trapped in this small northern Idaho town with heavy family obligations and no visible pathway to use for an escape.

The diving work had dried up and I was not a logger. There was no work in Orofino that would pay enough to meet living expenses and medical bills, let alone permit any saving for college. Because of my feelings of desperation, I had allowed myself to fall into a pool of self-pity.

One beautiful day in mid April Susan was visiting a couple of her friends and I was lying on the lawn in front of our apartment. The lawn beneath our living room window sloped down overlooking the town. To the left of Main Street, at the far end of town, I could see the bridge that leads from the state highway and crosses the Clearwater River into the other end of town. Sparsely wooded hills surrounded the town, and the river flowed along the highway at the base of the hills on one side and along the town on the other.

During the late summer months of August and September, the water level gets quite low and the river becomes crystal clear. Its white sand floor winds through huge rock structures, sculpted by the eroding force of fast-moving water. In mid to late August, the upper Clearwater becomes a chain of placid blue-green pools, linked together by white-water rapids. Spectacular white sand beaches border the entire length of the river from its headwaters down to Lewiston.

The river becomes a wonderful natural water playground during the summer months. Now the river level was very high and its upper tributaries were swollen with the melted snow from the surrounding mountains, filling the main Clearwater with silt, logs, and other debris.

At this time, the white sand beaches were underwater and the engorged river was running just a few feet below its banks.

Even though the river was high, muddy and wild, it was still beautiful in its setting of pine covered foothills. The way I was feeling at the moment even the beauty of the morning scene did little to still the unrest in my soul. I slid further and further into a dark mood and began to curse luck and circumstances. I was 26 years old and I seemed to be going nowhere!

I laid there for a time watching the river and I started to think up ways to escape from my perceived predicament. I was so frustrated I began to scheme. Then something my dad once told me scrolled through my mind. "The darkest day of a man's life is the day he sits down to plan how to get money without earning it." He also told me once, "If you don't like the game you're playing, change the game." OK, I thought, what game could I play with the board and pieces I had then? My current skill was limited to that of a trained deep-sea diver, and I had a passion for science, particularly medical science.

There seemed to be no way to fit the parts together. It was obvious that what I wanted was some way to combine medical science and diving. I thought of becoming a doctor, specializing in the area of submarine medicine, or diving physiology research, but given the status of my formal education the road seemed long and complicated.

First, I would have to go to college for an undergraduate degree and then get into medical school. The challenge seemed overwhelming; from my perspective as a 26-year-old, the time required to achieve that goal seemed like an eternity. Where could I get the money needed to attend college, let alone pay for medical school if I were accepted? Even if I got some money to get started, how could I support and raise my family and still devote the kind of time and intensity to such a demanding academic regimen? How was I going to get out of Orofino? At that moment I don't think I had enough gas money to drive the 44 miles to Lewiston.

I sat watching the fast flowing river passing under the Orofino Bridge on its way to the Pacific Ocean. Feeling trapped and over-whelmed, I said, "Maybe I'll have to swim out of Orofino down the Clearwater River." My words echoed in my mind, and for long moment, I stood staring at the river.

It's interesting how the human mind works after hatching an idea. My mind started asking itself questions. Could someone actually swim from Orofino, Idaho to the Pacific Ocean? How far was it? How long would it take? What are the dangers? Did I have physical stamina to do it? How could doing it help me achieve my goals? My mind was bombarded with its own questions!

The sudden, absurd prospect of actually swimming down the river to the sea obliterated all the depressed feelings I was having. It was somehow cathartic and it injected a new feeling of excitement in my veins. I rose from the lawn and went into the apartment. I couldn't purge the thought from my mind. How swimming from where I was to the Pacific Ocean could possibly be an answer to my needs was beyond me, but some unknown connection was subcon-sciously weaving a solution in my mind.

I knew quite a bit about the river between Orofino and Lewiston because I taught sports scuba diving to the area residents and we had made many dives in the deeper pools when the water was clear and the current was slow. Plagued by curiosity, I had to know the answers that I had posed to myself.

Over the next week I consulted all sources available to get the facts I needed. First, the distance from Orofino to Astoria traveling down the Clearwater, Snake, and Columbia Rivers was 557 miles.

Lewis and Clark made the trip by canoe in 32 days. They probably avoided some of the more dangerous rapids. Their journal mentioned the portage around Celilo Falls, which was 12 miles upriver from the present location of the Dalles Dam. The old falls was a popular Indian fishing site and was submerged by the creation of the reservoir behind the Dam. At least that was one less hazard to worry about if one were contemplating swimming down the Columbia. For the swim to have significance, I thought that swimming the distance in less time than Lewis and Clark took to make the trip by canoe would create a catchy challenge.

In order to make the trip in 31 days, one would have to swim 18 miles a day. There would be fast current in some parts of the river, but at that time there was still 186 miles of relatively still water in the reservoirs behind the dams. In some areas of the Snake and Columbia Rivers surface currents can be nullified by the fierce winds that roar up the Columbia and Snake River canyons. In the large lakes formed by the reservoirs you may find yourself swimming against wind driven surface current.

During the next three weeks I studied the probability of doing the swim. I got everything I could find on the river in the library. I wrote to the Corps of Engineers, the Bureau of Reclamation, and the Department of the Interior for Idaho, Washington, and Oregon to get detailed information on certain areas of the rivers. I called and talked to the sports fishing clubs in about 15 towns. I contacted boat captains that routinely tow barges up and down the river. I even talked with the Coast Guard and law enforcement teams that patrol the river in certain areas.

Over a period of three weeks I had collected a lot of information on what would be involved in making such a swim. I figured that anyone attempting this feat would have to exert the equivalent energy of swimming 16 miles a day in still water at a strong pace. The thought of swimming more than half the distance of the English Channel for 31 consecutive days was a showstopper. My buddies from the Orofino Boat and Dive Club told me that no one could do it, and that I would be crazy to try. I guess that meant expecting company on the swim was out of the question!

Over the next week, I recalculated the amount of help that the current would provide and then added the average swimming speed to the current's velocity. Due to the temperature and conditions of the river in midsummer, my calculations included using fins, mask, and snorkel, and a neoprene wet suit.

Taking into consideration the current, a moderate fin stroke, and floating rest periods, I figured that covering an average of 18 miles a day would require swimming more than 10 hours in the water each day. That kind of exposure to the water temperature for days and weeks at a time was a problem, so it would be necessary to have the thermal protection of the wet suit. In addition to thermal protection, the rubber suit when weighted lightly, would offer a certain amount of relaxing buoyancy.

Even if I could get some help from the current and keep from getting hypothermia, there was still the matter of physical conditioning and stamina required to pull this off. I was in good physical condition, never smoked, drank only on occasion, and was pretty strong for my size and weight, but I knew that to do this swim would require intense training and peak conditioning.

I had been focusing so much on the facts of the river swim, and the conditioning required, I hadn't considered any hazards or obstacles I might encounter on the swim. In the next two days, I contacted several people who were very knowledgeable about areas of the river and asked them about any hazards.

After I got that information from them, I had more weight on the "maybe it can't be done" side of the equation. There were places like Big Eddy on the Clearwater, the Riparia, Texas, and Palouse rapid chain, and the Lyons Ferry whirlpools were all within a 10-mile stretch on the Snake. One might encounter a storm on the lake reservoir behind the McNary Dam, and then there were stories about the "Devils Doorway" at "Hell's Gate" on the Columbia. There was also the small craft weather hazard potential in the lower Columbia, large amounts of boat traffic, and a high-level of pollutants in the water below Portland. All of this "encouraging" information didn't do much to bolster my confidence.

I had almost abandoned the idea of taking the challenge when I confided in a buddy of mine who was a disc jockey at the local radio station. He mentioned it to his station manager, and the station manager called a local public relations company that I will refer to as "EEE." The company was building a beautiful new structure and tourist facility at "Canoe Campsite." They were promoting Lewis and Clark and Nez Perce Indian historical mystique, and had big plans to draw thousands of tourists to the area during the summer months.

Two days later I received a phone call from the manager of EEE. He said he had heard about my interest in doing the river swim and would like to meet with me over breakfast to discuss the possibility of becoming a sponsor and public relations agent for the swim. I agreed to meet him the following morning and hung up the phone. I was more than a little surprised that anyone might be seriously interested in my crazy idea.

The next morning I arose early and told Susan that I had a breakfast meeting with someone to discuss a project I had in mind. I hadn't let Susan in on the nature of the project yet. At 8:00 a.m. I met the manager of EEE. He was a medium built man in a tan suit and black tie. He had short, coal black hair and wore Italian sunglasses. He introduced himself and told me his name. It sounded French; his first name started with the same letter as his last name. He had an air of suave arrogance about him, and when he pronounced his name it sounded as if he was announcing his own entrance to the Queen's Ball. He had dark piercing eyes and a direct mannerism. We ordered breakfast, and he began telling me about the E.E.E. Corporation's plans to put Orofino, Idaho on the map. They wanted to make it a tourist mecca for the entire United States!

He then started questioning me about the swim and whether or not it could be done. He was especially excited about the concept of challenging Lewis and Clark's time to reach Astoria; he was sure that EEE could promote it into a major national event! He reminded me that the Seattle's world's fair would open that summer and did I think I could complete the swim in time to make the opening? He envisioned he could make me a guest celebrity at the fair and get me offers for product endorsements that would pay big money. He asked me what I wanted if I could complete the swim successfully. I told him I would like to make enough money to go to college and eventually get into medical school.

For two hours after breakfast we continued talking about the possibility of doing the swim. He was very impressed with the detailed research I had done. By the time we finished talking he had me convinced that the swim was a worthwhile pursuit, and that with his help I could realize all my goals and dreams. When he got up from the table he said he was going back to his office to prepare a formal offer from EEE to be my agent.

I left the restaurant a little overwhelmed by the prospect. If he did actually make an offer, I realized I would have to make a commitment to do it, or forget it. I went back to the apartment and told Susan about the idea for the swim and the offer. I also told her what I had learned through my research about the difficulty of doing such a feat. When I finished, she was silent and stared at me for a long moment. I really expected her to tell me that it was a stupid idea, but instead a slight smile crept onto her lips and with a twinkle in her eye she said, "Go for it!"

I was amazed at her response. Here she was with one small child and pregnant with another. She was suffering from a chronic medical condition, her husband was barely making ends meet, and as if it were a decision to go to the movies, she tells me to "go for it." "I'm not sure I can do it," I said. "I would have to train, and get into ultra shape, even then, I'm not sure I could do it."

She walked up to me slowly, put her arms around my waist, and looked deep into my eyes as if she was searching my mind for answers. "You can do it!" she said with conviction. There was no more discussion. The decision had been made. I went to the phone and called EEE. The receptionist put me through to the manager. I told him that if he was serious about the offer to go ahead and write it up. I would do the swim.

CHAPTER 6

Preparation and Training

It was now the middle of April. In order to coincide with the world's fair festivities, the swim would have to start the first week in July and be completed by the first week of August. That gave me just two and a half months to train. Again, a wave of self-doubt overwhelmed me. There didn't seem to be enough time to prepare physically for a feat like the river swim. I would have to find a place to train and set up a training regimen as soon as possible.

I called my friend at the radio station to tell him that EEE had offered to sponsor the swim, and if the deal between us was satisfactory, I was going to do it. He was elated and wanted to know if he could break the news on his evening radio program. I said to hold off until EEE and I had a deal in writing, then he could break the news. I told him that I needed a place to work out. He said he knew Mr. Neuman, who owned the old Neuman lumber mill and that he had a private gym that was well equipped. He said he would talk to him about using it for my training. He also suggested that I talk to the Athletic Department at the high school about using some of their training facilities.

The next few weeks were a blur of activity. The contract with the EEE was signed. They were to sponsor me and take care of all the P.R. They agreed to pay me $10,000 on the successful completion of the swim and acquire additional sponsors for endorsements. I was to get seventy percent of any proceeds and endorsement earnings from the swim. EEE also agreed to replace my hospital salary for the month of June so I could train full time.

After the local radio announcement about the swim, the news spread quickly all over the small town. Since I was from Lewiston, only 44 miles away, the media there heard about the swim and called to get interviews. Mr. Neuman offered his private gym, and the coach at the high school said I could use whatever equipment I needed.

Physical fitness buffs and nutritionists from the local area who heard about the swim called me to offer diets and training tips. I thanked them for their advice, wrote down all their suggestions, and with some contributions from all of them, I developed my own training program.

EEE was concerned that I had to wear a partial plate to conceal a front tooth I had broken as a kid. A local dentist volunteered his services to fix it for me and a benefactor donated some money for the materials. The dentist wanted to install an experimental bridge with the work planned to be completed a week before the swim. Because of a delay in getting the bridge made, I wound up starting the swim with a temporary preparation in my mouth.

I started my training during the day while still working the night shift at the hospital. I worked out three times a week during the first two weeks and four times a week for the next two weeks. I intensified my training to six times a week in the last week of May. I pushed the training a little too hard during those first few weeks and my body really rebelled. After about the fourth week of training I begin to get seasoned into the routine.

The first of June I left the hospital and started full time training.

EEE had arranged some publicity to promote the swim so I had to take a couple of days out of my training to do some promotion. We

Robert Smiley and US Senator Frank Church. The Governor gave me a new pair of fins to use on the swim and a miniature Idaho State flag to present Oregon State officials when I arrived in Astoria. I wasn't happy about the break in my training but I knew it was necessary if we were to capitalize on the event.

By the middle of June, I had gained 15 lbs. of solid muscle. I weighed 160 lbs and my daily training schedule went something like this.

Morning: Eat a modest breakfast and jog about three miles out to Neuman's mill to work out in the gym. There I did two hours of free weight and exercise training, then 30 minutes of punching a heavy speed bag with five pound weights in each hand. After the gym work out, I ran two miles to the high school and worked out for another two hours on the trampoline and flying rings. After the morning work out, I would run from the school into town and up the steep Canada Hill to the apartment for lunch. After eating, I rested for about forty-five minutes. Afternoon: Run from the apartment to the high school stadium and work out there. Friends and relatives would meet me at the stadium and throw a football for me while I ran out for passes. It was a great way to run a lot of wind sprints without becoming too bored. After the wind sprints, I would run back up Canada Hill to the apartment, load my swimming gear in the car, and go pick up a friend who had volunteered to help me train.

We would drive up the North Fork of the Clearwater River. (This was before the Dawarshak Dam was built, and it was a fast moving river, instead of 60 miles of lake reservoir as it is today). I would dress into my wet suit, put on fins, mask, and snorkel and swim in place against a slow moving current for about one and a half hours. After that, I would swim down the river for six or seven miles through alternating stretches of swift current, slow moving pools, and white water rapids. My friend would drive the car along the river road and monitor me while I was in the river. Sometimes I would swim another half hour against the current if I wasn't too tired.

When the day's workout was done, I would go home for supper and about an hour's rest. After supper, I would run down the hill and jog through the streets of town; then I would run back up the hill to the apartment. I would spend some time with Susan and my son, Ron, and then go to bed pretty early.

By the last week in June most of the merchants and townspeople knew who I was, and all about the swim. They would try to hand me stuff, give me high fives, and cheer me on as I did my evening runs. It was encouraging and rewarding to have so many people pulling for me. Looking back it reminds me of scenes from the *Rocky* movies when he was cheered on by the people of his neighborhood while he did his road work.

The training was intense, and I took two days off each week to let my system rebuild. I staggered my days off, so my body wouldn't get used to the workout routine. Funny thing about the human body; no matter how hard the physical demands of a workout, it always figures out a way to meet those demands with as little effort and pain as possible. The training was going great, and my strength and stamina was increasing dramatically each day! I was burning a lot of calories, but I was eating well and feeling good.

One night about three weeks before the swim, Susan and I were lying in bed talking. When we were ready to sleep Susan turned out the table lamp at the side of the bed. After the light was out, she swung her arm over toward me to give me a hug just as I lifted up to adjust my pillow. Her hand collided with my head and her fingernail went into my right eye! For a few seconds I felt a blinding pain and I rolled off the bed in agony. Susan tried to comfort me, but it felt like someone had thrown scalding hot sand into my eye.

The pain did not let up and two and a half hours later we wound ~~up at the local hospital emergency room.~~ The doctor on duty put

the morning I went to see an eye doctor. He said I had a pretty bad abrasion on the cornea and he did some work on it after giving me some more anesthetic.

He told me that the work he did on my eye would cause me some trauma over the next few days. The doctor gave me some drops to combat the pain and told me to wear a patch over the eye until it healed.

Boy, what luck! There was only three weeks left before the swim was to start and I injure an eye. For the next two days, I wore the patch. There was some pain and spatial disorientation and I couldn't train. I couldn't afford to miss any days of training, so I counted my two days of convalescing as my two rest days. On the third and fourth day I did my whole training routine and doubled up my gym workouts because I couldn't get in the water. On the fifth day I took off the patch, and did a full day's workout including a ten mile river swim. My eye healed rapidly and within a week I had two good eyes again.

During the last two weeks of training my brother, Bill, worked out with me, and joined me on the afternoon river swims. Susan's brother, John Craig, was to join us during the last week of training and the two of them would act as my safety divers on the big swim. Both John and Bill were trained scuba divers and excellent swimmers.

We had planned to kick off the swim the morning of the Fourth of July to start the City's annual celebration, but the manager of EEE was getting nervous about the 31 day target and pressed us to start the swim on July 2nd. The dignitaries of the town were a little upset that the start of the swim would not kick off the city's Fourth of July celebration, but they said they would provide an official send off for us on July 2nd.

I was assured that Susan and my son would be taken care of during the swim. Her folks were bringing John down to train with us that last week before the swim. They planned to stay in Orofino for the start of the swim and then take Susan and my son, Ron, back to Spokane for the days I was going to be swimming down the river.

EEE had contracted for a jet boat owned by Hell's Canyon Excursions to accompany me on the swim. They called the boat the *No-Name,* and its pilot was a young guy by the name of King Cole. John, Bill, King Cole, and I would make up the marathon swim team. The local Boat and Dive Club presented us with a large diving flag mounted on a six-foot mast that we could use to warn other boaters that there was a diver in the water near our boat.

The Coast Guard had the swim schedule and would post a notice to mariners on a daily basis to let boaters sailing the river know my general location. We also sent notices and our planned schedule to water sports operators along the river route.

Two days before the swim was to begin, King Cole arrived with the jet boat. He was a tall, thin, young man with a great attitude and a keen sense of humor. He had been running the boat for Floyd Harvey, owner of "Hell's Canyon Excursions." King had lots of experience running tourists up through desolate, rough, wild stretches of the Snake River into Hell's Canyon. He was excited about the swim, and we were glad to have him as our skipper. King and I worked out our operating plan and then we took the boat out into the Clearwater River to practice some operating and emergency procedures.

With one day to go EEE's manager assured me that the Mead Dalton Company and the Wyler Watch Company were secured as sponsors and that he had several other deals in the works. He said that Mayor, Burt Curtis and the town of Orofino were planning a big send off at 9:00 a.m. on the 2nd of July. He asked if the team would be ready to start the swim by the 2nd; I assured him that we would be ready.

There were several more meetings and a number of things to do before final preparations for the swim were complete. My dentist said he had arranged to use the office of a colleague in Clarkston to install my bridge the evening of the first day of the swim. That was the best plan he could come up with because the bridge would not be ready until then. This meant that after swimming fifty miles I would have to spend about three hours in a dental chair undergoing a bridge installation. I dreaded the idea, but there was no other option.

The night before the start of the swim I was showing some anxiety. I knew I should get to bed and rest as much as possible, but I just could not get to sleep. I tried not to think of anything more than the swim I had to make the first day. I would worry about the rest of the swim in sequence. The first day we were planning to go 48 miles down the Clearwater to Lewiston to the Washington Water Power Dam.

Lewiston was my hometown. There would be media coverage on my arrival, and the Junior Chamber of Commerce was to host a dinner that night for me at the Lewis and Clark hotel. I couldn't help but think about the number of people who might be planning to attend that dinner. What if I ruined all their plans by not being able to complete the first 48 miles in time. Preconceived problems were haunting me!

About 11 p.m. I got up and went to the living room couch. I sat there looking out over the lights of Orofino. During the past few days the weather had been perfect with long sunny days and warm star-filled nights. The scene from our living room was like an artist rendering of a perfect night in a rural mountain town. There was a huge moon hanging over the hills east of town and I could see the moonlight reflecting from sections of the river below the pine-covered hills. It highlighted the surface texture of the water flowing westward toward the sea. Tomorrow I would be in that water all day.

I sat there in the dark, staring out the window, and then I heard

Susan's soft footsteps as she walked around to the back of the couch behind me. "Are you worried?" she asked. "I'm afraid I won't be able to do it," I said. "What if I disappoint everyone, and make a fool of myself?" She was silent for a few moments, and then she said, "Spence, at least you have the guts to try! How many other people do you know that have announced to the world that they are going to swim down three rivers totaling 557 miles in less than 32 days?"

"You have only one person to satisfy with this challenge; that person is you. No one else can take the blame if you fail, but no one else can take the credit if you succeed." She put her warm arms around my shoulders and gave me a big hug and a kiss on the back of the neck. Then she said, "If anyone can do it, you can—but you're going to fall asleep in the middle of the river tomorrow if you don't get some rest!" Then, she walked back into our bedroom.

I sat quietly for a few more minutes digesting her words and then I got up and went to our room. As I passed my son's crib, I bent down and whispered, "Boy, it's a good thing you're too young to understand what your crazy dad is about to try." I kissed his soft little cheek and went to bed. I put my arm around Susan and gave her a gentle squeeze. She chuckled softly and said, "Go to sleep."

The alarm went off at 6:00 a.m. and my first thoughts were to get up and get out to the gym. Then I became fully awake. There was no more training; the swim starts today! I got up, dressed and ate a light breakfast. I packed my suitcase with clothes and things I would need after each day's swim. I also took a journal with the resolve to write in it at the end of each day. By eight o'clock I was ready and I told Susan to drive to the staging area at the river and that I would walk there.

It was a beautiful morning, perfect for the start of the swim. Most of the stores were just opening as I walked down the hill and through the main street of town. Some of the shops had signs in windows and on their marquees wishing me well. People came out to shake hands, or give a high five, as I passed by.

I reached the staging area about 8:20 a.m. and used a small shed adjacent to the staging site to dress into my wet suit. Bill and John were already in their suits and were waiting in the boat which was beached at the site. I was amazed at the number of people that started to gather!

By 8:45 a.m all the town dignitaries, a lot of my friends, and the send-off crowd were gathered at the beach. The mayor addressed the crowd. He gave a speech about civic pride and complimented the people on their support. He gave me a gold nugget in a small vial that I was to present to the mayor of Astoria. The golden nugget was symbolic of the town of Orofino, which in Spanish means, "fine gold."

The mayor asked me to speak. I thanked all the people for their support and asked them to keep me in their prayers. When I was through I shook the mayor's hand and waved to all my friends. I gave Susan and my son a last minute hug, walked down to the beach, and got into the jet boat.

King Cole eased the *No-Name* out into the river. We turned and traveled about 100 yards upstream from the Orofino Bridge. I put on my fins, mask, and snorkel and stretched out along the railing at side of the boat so I would be facing the town and the crowd at the staging area. King swung the bow downstream and opened the throttle. We approached the Bridge doing about 25 knots. Just as we passed under the bridge I did a roll entry off the side of the boat. It was kind of a flashy start—just the way we rehearsed it!

The water washed over me and when the inertia was spent I broke to the surface to hear cheers from a crowd of people that had gathered on the bridge. People were yelling and waving from the bank as I passed the crowd at the staging area. I raised my arm and waved to everyone. The swim was on!

A mile or so out of Orofino we passed State Hospital North where I worked as a Psychiatric Aide. There were a few patients and attendants outside on the park-like grounds. A few of the attendants must have been watching for me and they waved as we passed by.

The mental hospital was a group of large brick buildings situated on a timbered hillside overlooking the Clearwater River. The grounds were well manicured with shrubs and lawns. Having worked in several areas of the hospital, I couldn't help thinking about the poor souls inside, prisoners of their mental afflictions. I was an attendant long enough to develop a lot of empathy for them. During the next mile I tried to get the hospital out of my thoughts, but persistent recollections of my experiences there produced some vivid memories.

CHAPTER 7

The Ward

There were many incidents and experiences in the months I served as the night shift supervisor for the men's receiving ward, but one night is indelibly imprinted in my memory. It was about 11 p.m. when the administration office called the ward to advise me that the midnight shift crew was returning from Lewiston, about 44 miles away, and their car had broken down about halfway to Orofino.

They had called someone to come and get them, but it would be a couple of hours before they could get to the hospital. Administration told me I would have to cover the ward until they got there. I told them no problem and informed my assistant that we were on overtime.

It was a Friday night, and he and his wife were planning to drive to Spokane for the weekend for a reunion with his family. They had planned to leave as soon as he was off duty. A two-hour delay would mean that they wouldn't get to Spokane until the wee hours of the morning. All the patients were in bed, problem patients were locked secure in their rooms, and I figured it would only be an hour or two before the other crew got there. Because everyone was asleep, and the ward had been extremely quiet at night for the past week, I told my assistant he could go home.

After he left, I stayed in the ward office until it was time to make rounds at 12:30. We always made rounds with two attendants, but I felt I could handle most situations that might arise, and there were a couple of patients in the open wing that I could depend on to help me if I needed assistance.

I took my flashlight from the ward office and started my rounds. I went to the end of the hall where all the problem patients were kept locked in their rooms and began crosschecking each room by looking in through the small wire grid windows. I checked each room and all of the patients were in bed sleeping soundly.

Only one room contained a potentially dangerous patient; he was a tall, muscular guy about six-foot six and weighed about 260 pounds. He could be a real threat at times, but he seemed to like me for some reason and he was never hostile toward me.

When I reached his room, I swung the flashlight up to the small window and put my face up close to check on him. Two huge, angry-looking eyes were staring back at me and as my light hit his face I could see that he was not a happy man! He glared at me menacingly through the small window and then he slammed his huge hand against the door with a thunderous bang. It actually shook the door, forcing me to jump back in surprised shock. He pounded on the door several more times and I was afraid he would wake up other patients in the locked rooms.

Realizing that I had startled him when I thrust my light into his face, I came up with an idea. I stood a few feet away from the window and shined the flashlight on my face and tried to force a smile. Almost instantly his pounding stopped. I kept the light on my face for a few moments and then I slowly moved up to look in the window. He had moved back about 4 feet from the door, and as the light hit him I saw a big toothy grin on his face; he was giving me the OK sign! My heart began receding from my throat to its original position and slowed to a somewhat normal beat.

Rounds were over and I returned to the office. I called the administration desk and reported that all was well on the ward. I also informed them that I was alone on the ward. It was now 1:00 a.m. and I asked whether they had heard from the night shift crew, they had not. I was now secure in the wardroom office and was not really looking forward to the next security round!

About 1:30 p.m. the phone rang. It was administration informing me that the State Police had arrived with a new admittance and that they would be bringing him up to the ward in about 15 minutes. A moment after I hung up, the State Police part finally sunk in. I redialed administration, but the line was busy. About 10 minutes later the buzzer sounded from the main ward door and I answered the intercom. "This is Sergeant Jordan of the Idaho State Patrol. We have a patient."

I looked down the hall to the main door and I could see movement through the small window. Hospital Security opened the ward door for the police and two tall, husky State Police officers pushed a medium build, dark-haired man in his mid-fifties through the door. One officer held the man by the shoulder while the other unlocked a pair of handcuffs, that had one wrist secured to the back of his belt.

When they freed the man and stepped away I could see why only one hand was cuffed. His other arm was heavily bandaged from the forearm down and I could see that his left hand was missing. The two officers secured the restraint equipment and without a word they were out the door. Their entrance and hasty deposit of the patient was so abrupt I hadn't had time to leave the ward office.

I could still hear the muffled voices of the officers talking to our security people outside the ward door. Suddenly, a cold chill ran up my spine and I quickly pushed the intercom button. "Officers." I called, "This is the ward supervisor. Can you tell me what we have here?" There was a momentary pause, and then the Sergeant's deep voice said calmly, "About three o'clock yesterday afternoon, he killed his wife with an axe and then cut off his hand." As his words faded, my mind reeled! I started to ask him about the man's current mental state, but I could hear the outside door open and close. They were gone before I could get the words out!

The Police and Security officers were gone and 30 yards away, standing mute by the door, was a man who had done something I couldn't even imagine. I eased the office door closed and turned the lock. There was no immediate threat to me, but the problem was what to do with the man standing down the hall. I picked up the phone and called administration.

The lady on night shift duty was a seasoned veteran at her job and had seen it all. I apprised her of the situation and asked about the midnight shift crew. She said she hadn't heard from them since their first call and then she asked about the man. "He's standing in the open ward hall by the main door and hasn't moved a muscle since the police took the cuffs off of him," I said. "Well," she replied in a voice that sounded matter-of-fact and a little nonchalant, "You're strong, go get the man and put him in a locked room. I'll call you when the other crew gets here." Then she hung up. I just stood there for a couple of minutes holding the dead phone to my ear wondering how many axe murderers she had admitted during her 14 years on the job. At that moment I would have gladly traded my situation for a broken leg!

I knew I had to do something to get the man into one of the locked rooms. Even though I had dealt with a large variety of mental patients both placid and volatile, I wasn't sure how to approach someone who had committed such a gory act. Nothing had changed. He still stood frozen in place where the police had left him. Before the police brought him up to the ward, I was brewing some fresh coffee. Now the sound of it's steady percolation drummed an idea into my mind.

I composed myself, opened the office door, stepped out into the hallway and faced the man. In the most relaxed and confident a voice I could muster I said, "They tell me you've had one hell of a time; I bet you could use a cup of fresh coffee." There was no response. He just stood there, slightly swaying on his feet and I braced myself for some sort of outburst or reaction—there was none. I turned and walked into the office, grabbed one of our more comfortable office chairs and drug it out into the hall.

I set a medicine stand next to the chair and put a hot steaming cup of coffee on the stand. I turned to the man and said, "The coffee's good. I just made it. Come, sit down and have a cup. No one is going to hassle you."

Then I entered the office, closed the bottom half of the Dutch door and locked it. I sat down at the office desk and forced myself through some duties, trying to act unconcerned about the axe murderer loose in my ward.

About six minutes passed, and I heard shuffling footsteps coming down the hall toward the office. I tried not to react, but I cast a quick glance in the direction of the footsteps. I tried to act busy with my ward paperwork, and I could tell that he was just outside the office door. I heard him ease himself into the chair and the sound of the coffee cup being dragged toward him and then I heard him take a couple of sips. Slowly, I stood up, turned and went to the door.

 He was a medium built man and wore a pair of khaki pants and a pullover type sweatshirt. There were splotches of blood on his clothes. He had a couple of days growth on his face, but he did not look at all sinister. He just looked confused and disheveled. I stood in the doorway and he looked up at me. His eyes were sad and he looked very tired.

I'm sure they had sedated him heavily after his arrest. He forced a feeble smile and said, "The coffee is good—thanks." Suddenly, all the apprehension left me and I asked him if his arm was hurting; did he need anything for it? He said "No, God had told him to cut it off and it didn't hurt much." I didn't know how to respond to that so I just nodded my head and said, "Let me know if you need anything."

I returned to my desk and the office and waited until he finished his coffee; then I stood up and went to the door. "I'll bet you could use some sleep," I said. He looked up at me and nodded. I opened the office door, locked it behind me, and walked up to the man. I offered him my arm to help him up from the chair. He took it and stood up. I escorted him down the hallway to an empty room. I turned on the light and helped him to the bed. He said he could manage with his clothes and I turned to leave.

Before I turned off the light, I said. "We have some strange patients here that might try to come into your room and bother you. I'll lock the door so no one can get in. You have a call button by your bed if you need anything." He acknowledged with a wave and then pushed himself up onto the bed. I turned out the light, closed and locked the door. A tremendous feeling of total relaxation and satisfaction came over me at that time. I conducted my rounds and then returned to the office.

I had just sat down at the desk when the main ward door opened and the long overdue midnight crew arrived. We conducted our briefing and medication count and I told them about my evening's experience. They were impressed. As I drove home that night I couldn't get the man out of my mind. It was natural to be reviled and repulsed by his crime, but there was something strange and pathetic about him. It left me wondering what sort of images, voices, and urges must be coursing through his tortured mind.

When I got home I checked on Ronnie asleep in his crib and climbed into bed. Susan woke up and gave me a warm, strong hug.

The night's bizarre events faded into normal dreams and I woke up in the morning to a new day and a new life.

CHAPTER 8

The Clearwater

eaving Orofino behind, we struck out downriver for Lewiston. We passed a few scattered groups of fans at Canoe Camp-Site, a couple of miles below Orofino. This was the place where Lewis and Clark, and the Indian princess, Sacagawea, started their trip down the river to Astoria. Looking down the long stretch of river that disappeared between rolling hills, I wondered what went through their minds as they started on the same journey I was about to make?

If there were any more fans in the next 10 miles, I didn't see them because the river was now demanding my full attention. The current was pretty fast, and it wove its way downstream in a convoluted path of branching channels. The water in some of the channels was too shallow and rough to swim through. My crew would scout ahead in the boat and point out which side of the river I should swim through in order to have the easiest and safest path. Going through the wrong side might cause serious injury and end the swim with a trip to the hospital, or worse.

About 15 miles and 12 channels into the swim, I came to a couple of painful realizations. First, there was going to be a lot of extra swimming required to get into the safest channels because the river could be one quarter mile wide or more in some places. Second, it appeared as if God had staggered the safest channels alternately on opposite sides of the river. That epiphany was not encouraging and was definitely not factored into my river swim analysis. During the next hour, I realized that my planned "current ride" down this first 48 miles of river was going to turn into real work.

The Clearwater River was much colder than usual for that time of the year and about three hours into the swim I began to experience severe abdominal muscle cramps. The pain was continuous and got so severe that I wasn't able to swim fast enough to avoid the dangerous channels. After I accidentally entered a stretch of nasty rapids (which my safety boat had to circumnavigate) I experienced such excruciating cramps that I didn't think I would be able to continue.

Fortunately, I entered relatively smooth water flowing downstream at a nice pace. I signaled my safety boat crew that I was in trouble and in a few seconds the boat was alongside. I told them about the severe cramping and they could see that I was in a lot of pain. I knew if I got out of the water before I had completed my day's distance I would be admitting defeat and forfeiting the challenge. There was no way I wanted to quit, but I couldn't stand the paralyzing pain in my stomach.

My crew put the rope ladder over the side to help me climb into the boat. I was almost in tears as I put my fin on the bottom rung of the ladder and started to pull myself up into the boat. The moment I put some weight on my foot, I felt an immediate relief from the cramps. "Wait!" I said. "The cramps are leaving. I'm going to keep part of my weight on the ladder as we float along here for a few minutes and see what happens."

About 10 minutes later, the cramps had diminished significantly and I had an idea. I thought if I could get some sort of weight or resistance against my abdominal muscles, it might alleviate the cramping situation. I asked the crew to go to the beach and find me a two-foot long driftwood log about six inches in diameter.

I stepped off the ladder, pushed away from the boat, and the crew drove off toward the beach. By the time they got back with the log the cramps were starting again. I straddled the small log and the buoyancy of the log pushing upward against my stomach provided just enough pressure to counteract the cramping.

With the log beneath me, I could still swim using my arms to paddle along while the log pushed some weight against my abdomen. I kept the log between my legs for about an hour and the cramping stopped. I had the crew pick up the log and keep it in case I needed it again.

I was feeling much better now and more confident about avoiding failure. I asked the boat crew for a can of nutritional supplement called "Nutriment" that had been supplied by the Mead Dalton Co. The cramping did not return and fortunately there were no serious rapids to swim through during my recovery period. John and Bill would swim along with me in areas where the river was docile, or there were moderate rapids.

We had seen only a few scattered groups of fans along the river, but when we passed under the Lenore Bridge we saw a fairly large number of people taking pictures. We thought some of them might have been from the media. I knew that we were getting close to "Big Eddy," where the river makes a sharp bend one way and then turns sharply the other way. The switch back effect of the fast river in that area created a huge area of swirling currents. Any attempt to swim through the eddy could be thwarted by the circling, back-flowing surface currents.

It seemed like only a few minutes had passed when the crew came alongside and announced that "Big Eddy" was about 300 yards ahead. I thanked God that the cramps were gone. Having at least temporarily overcome my first adversary, (the unexpected cramps), I got ready to do battle with my second adversary, "Big Eddy."

The speed of the current increased dramatically as we got within 100 yards of the Eddy. As I entered the first bend, the river was really moving. I could hear the roar of the rolling water and I begin to feel weird undulations of the current on my legs. I knew that as I approached the switch back corner of the Eddy I would meet a spiraling centrifuge of current trying to repel me back upstream and into a maelstrom of suck holes and turbulent water. When I was within 20 yards of the second bend, I could feel a strong current pushing me back. I was within 10 yards of the sharp bend that turned downriver when I lost the battle and was swept out into the back flowing water and propelled about 40 yards upstream.

My next attempt to get around the corner was foiled again by the swirling back-eddy currents. This time I was pulled out into an area of suck holes and large whirlpools. Ten minutes later I was still going around in circles in the middle of the river fighting with the currents.

With some hard swimming, I got close enough to the riverbank to make another attempt to round the corner. My crew in the safety boat was getting concerned, and they were also having difficulty maneuvering in the turbulent water. By this time I had cycled upstream far enough to get a little rest from the hard swimming in the back-eddy and whirlpools.

I let the water carry me toward the second bend and when I began to feel the current pushing against me, I started swimming as hard as I could.

The current was so strong that even against my maximum effort it propelled me sideways and forced me into shallow water about five yards from shore. That turned out to be a blessing in disguise.

The current in the shallow water was much weaker, but still deep enough for me to swim. The flow against me was strong, but by swimming hard in about four feet of water, I was able to break through the back-eddy into the slow-moving water on the downstream side of the bend. After rounding the bend, a strong downstream current swept me out into the main flow of the river. I was now passed "Big Eddy," and again on my way toward Lewiston.

In the next 10 miles we experienced a mix of alternating channels, rapids, and slow moving pools. It was now three o'clock, and I had been in the river for six hours. We were about 16 miles from the Washington Water Power Dam in Lewiston where I would end the first day's swim.

The last 14 miles of the river was relatively straight, with a slow steady current and a few channels, but no serious rapids. During this stretch of river Bill and John came in and swam with me again. When we got within nine miles of the dam at Lewiston the water really slowed down and the last eight miles became a narrow, placid lake of very slow moving water. The river here widened out into a reservoir just above the dam.

The south side of the reservoir was cordoned off by a large log-boom; that section of the river was known as the millpond. Inside the boom floated hundreds of pine logs waiting to be turned into raw lumber and paper at the Potlatch Forest Inc. mill.

Swimming those last few miles became a painful task. The slow loss of body heat and the fatigue of the day's swimming began to take its toll. My dental preparation had held up pretty well, but every time I clamped down on the mouthpiece of the snorkel I couldn't help but think of the dental work that would have to be done later that night.

The last four miles to the dam proved to be a physical and mental challenge. I could feel the material lining inside of the rubber wetsuit chafing the inside of the bends of my elbows and knees, making it increasingly painful to swim. During the last two miles I knew that I was doing serious damage to my flesh in those areas.

I swam to within a few hundred yards of the dam and I could see dozens of people on the bank of the river by the highway. As I got closer, I saw newspaper and TV cameramen and a welcoming committee, which included my wife and son. They were standing near the area where I was expected to exit. I swam up and touched the wall of the dam, then swam over to the landing site. I was exhausted, but very glad that I had made my first day's goal. It was nearly 6:00 p.m. when I reached the landing area. I had been swimming for eight hours and fifty minutes since we left Orofino.

Bill and John helped me from the water and up the bank. It was somewhat difficult to climb due to the pain from the raw areas on my body. I was also a little off balance from the constant rolling motion of the swim, that affected my equilibrium, like it does with sailors coming off ship after weeks at sea.

I reached the top of the bank to a cheering crowd, honking horns and lots of handshaking and hugs from friends and family. I momentarily forgot the pain and exhaustion. Then one of the reporters pointed at me and said "Hey! You're bleeding!" I looked down at my hands and they were dripping blood; then I saw that there was fresh blood pooling on my wetsuit boots.

Everyone got really excited and wanted to call for an ambulance. I said I was pretty sure it was from the chafing of the suit and that I was OK. My crew and sponsors insisted that I go to the hotel immediately and get some medical attention. I thanked the welcoming crowd for their support then waved to all of them as I got into a courtesy car with my family. After eight hours and fifty minutes of swimming and battling the Clearwater the first 48 miles of river was behind me, just 509 more to go starting the next morning.

We arrived at the Lewis and Clark Hotel where we were to stay and they were holding the reception dinner for me. First, I saw a doctor who treated my lacerations. He told me I couldn't sustain any more damage to those areas and that he was concerned about infection. To prevent more chafing we decided to cut out circular areas of the wetsuit where the chafing was causing problems. He decided we should medicate and coat the wounds with petroleum jelly before each day's swim. The doctor made me promise to clean the areas often and keep a close watch on the wounds for signs of infection.

The reception dinner and festivities were great. It felt good to receive such support from my hometown. I was proud to be from a town as gracious as Lewiston. The activities were over by 10:00 p.m. By 11:00 p.m. I was in Clarkston at the dental clinic of my dentist's friend and colleague. The installation of the bridge took more time than I expected because the bridge required some modifications. I was dead tired, and with the help of some nitrous oxide, I was able to doze through some of the procedure.

The excitement of the first day of the swim and the great reception I received from my hometown seemed to dictate my subconscious thoughts. While in the semi-conscious state induced by the nitrous oxide, I drifted back in time to my early years in Lewiston.

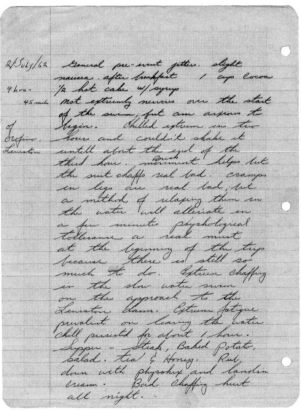

Page from the Swim Journal

CHAPTER 9

Shangri-La

It was about a two-hour winter drive from the ranch in Princeton to the top of the Lewiston hill. There was two feet of snow on top of the steep grade, which drops nine miles down into the Lewis and Clark Valley. Lewiston, Idaho and Clarkston, Washington are located where the Clearwater and Snake rivers meet, and define the border between Idaho and Washington. The towns of Lewiston and Clarkston derive their names from the famous explorers, Lewis and Clark. At that time, all the higher elevations around the valley were covered with deep snow, but the valley below looked green and lush because of an unusually warm climate. They actually call the valley, "The Banana Belt." My dad stopped our Conestoga ford wagon at a scenic pullout at the top of the grade and we got out to look down on our new hometown.

The contrast between the deep white snows that surrounded us and the spring-like appearance of the town below prompted my dad to comment that it reminded him of Shangri-La—a secret mystical place high in the Himalayan Mountains where there was eternal spring and no one aged as long as you stayed in Shangri-La. It was my Dad's Shangri-La!

The trip down the Lewiston grade was exciting, to say the least. The old Lewiston grade was notorious and had claimed its share of motorists. Thank God the snow was wet and mostly melted on the road, but the grade was treacherous with many hairpin turns and steep banks. There were some icy stretches and the little Model A Ford slid sideways several times on the way down. The grade drops from over 3000 ft. to about 800 ft. in a very short span. The trip down was scary, and my stepmother was freaked out. By the time we got off the grade and into the outskirts of town Lewiston became my Shangri-La, too!

My dad had arranged for us to stay at a small motel off Main Street until he could find a home for us. I was enrolled in a nearby grade school, and could easily walk the short six blocks to school in sunshine. For the next couple of weeks the weather was incredible, and I half believed this might really be Shangri-La!! I remember the beautiful fall colors and the classroom decorations for Thanksgiving; orange and black crepe paper, pumpkins, corn stocks, and horns of plenty. There were colorful pictures of turkeys with their tail feathers ruffled out and that orange gobbler-like thing hanging down from their neck. I still hated the milk people's Tom Turkey, but I had to admit they were colorful when alive, and tasted good when dead and roasted.

There's something special about the colors, smells, and feelings of fall. There were Thanksgiving, and Halloween decorations and the pleasant festive feeling. I can still see the large rust colored leaves blowing in the cold fall wind and feel the warmth of the steam radiators in our classroom. I remember the smiles from our gentle and kind teachers, and the bubbly enthusiasm of the children in my school when we had art class or recess. It was a carefree time for children then.

We stayed in the motel for about two months, then we moved to East Lewiston to a trailer court with small cabins on the banks of Lindsay Creek. The trailer court was owned by a kindly, old, white-haired lady who was confined to a wheelchair. They called her Auntie Miller. Her daughter, Esther had a son my age named Billy. He was a street-smart kid who always had an angle. At any given time Billy had a half dozen schemes working! He loved to play practical jokes on everyone, and sometimes I hated him when he played them on me. Most of the time I really liked Billy, and we were great friends.

The east end of Lewiston stared at Our Lady of Lourdes catholic church on Main Street and ended at the Lewiston Stockyards. If you went any further you would wind up at the Potlatch Forest Inc. Mill. It was the largest white pine mill in the world. Most of the population of the city worked at the lumber mill, the paper mill, food canneries, or were seasonal farm workers. The far end of Lewiston, where we lived, was a small community centered around three taverns, a small hotel, and a Phillips 66 gas station.

The kids that lived in East Lewiston were mostly the sons and daughters of mill workers, and the ones further up Lindsay Creek lived on small farms. Two blocks from the trailer court where we lived the main road forked left to the stockyards; the fork to the right went up Lindsay Creek.

Another family of Campbell's lived just across from us. Jack Campbell was the owner of Campbell's tavern. The fork in the road at the end of Main Street was known as Campbell's Corner. I kind of liked that! My dad liked to frequent Campbell's tavern on Saturdays, visit with his friends, tell stories, and gamble on pull-tabs. He was always pleasant to everyone, and everyone seemed to like him. My father did like to drink a few beers on his day off, but in all my young life I never saw him drunk or out-of-control.

The East Lewiston kids had somewhat of an unearned and tough reputation. To be accepted by the kids in our neighborhood, you had to endure some rites of passage. As an "east end kid," you had to hang out with the gang, but the east end gang of Lewiston, Idaho in 1947 was by no stretch of the imagination like the youth gangs of today's urban cities.

We were just kids with a lot of pent-up energy. When traveling with the pack language could get a little rough, but our worst language wouldn't compare to the normal dialogue in most current R-rated movies. We had kind of a kid code of conduct, which shunned stealing anything more valuable than a few apples from a local orchard or something like that.

All the kids I grew up with addressed adults as Sir and Ma'am and disrespect for elders wasn't tolerated. The parents in our neighborhood had an unwritten law. If any parent caught one of us doing something morally, or sociably unacceptable, they were allowed to discipline us just like we were their own children. It was like having parents watching you all over the neighborhood. Upon learning that some parent had to give us a swat; our parents would give us another swat when we got home.

We were definitely not a bunch of little angels. We did lots of things considered kid pranks at that time, which could be considered malicious mischief in today's judicial system. Some of the stupid things we did were downright dangerous, and most of our parents would have died if they had known the risks we took!

Our house was two blocks from the railroad yards and about four blocks from the stockyards. The stockyards had an old caretaker by the name of Jess. Jess was a nice old guy with whiskers, and everybody liked him, but we gave him fits by sneaking into the stockyard pens and trying to ride the cows. We would also sneak into the big hay barn and build forts and tunnels with the hay bales. Almost no one in our gang smoked, but Jess was afraid that one of us might set the hay on fire and burn up the stockyards—but no one ever did!

Nearly every Saturday there was a huge auction and farmers would come from all over the area to buy animals. The auctioneer would rattle off his spiel from the auctioneer booth and the ranchers and farmers would try to act totally uninterested. Periodically, they would give a hand, or head signal, that entered their bid. I watched them for hours and I could never figure out how they knew what the auctioneer was saying, or how they knew how much money they were bidding. Finally, the auctioneer would point at someone and say, "sold". That was the only time I knew for sure who bought the horse or the cow!

Watching the auction was almost as good as going to the movies. There was a whole cast of characters at every auction, and sometimes a drunk would get into the act and be quite entertaining until a couple of cowboys hired as bouncers would tackle him and carry him off. It seemed at that time very few people sued anyone for anything, particularly when they had suffered a consequence as a result of their own actions.

The cowboys would just lock the drunk in a horse stall. He would pass out, sleep it off, and when he woke up apologize to everyone for making an ass out of himself; then it was forgotten. In those days no one seemed to think that we should get the Supreme Court involved when people made fools of themselves.

There were four distinct seasons in Lewiston, and our gang of east end kids had special extracurricular activities for every season. In the spring, we would have dirt clod fights. In the hot summer, we threw water filled balloons at everything that moved. We would go down to the Mill Pond and swim in the Clearwater River and we took coal oil lanterns out to Mill Pond at night and fished for catfish. In the fall, the throwing weapon of choice was rotten fruit or vegetables, salvaged from neighborhood gardens. Sometimes, it would hurt to get hit with a partially rotten squash, but most of the time it was just messy and smelled bad! In the winter, it was snowballs. We threw them at everything, but mostly cars.

I can distinctly remember four events from our usual bag of pranks and shenanigans. One was the summer we decided to try to steal some grapes from the Tumelson's place up on Lindsay Creek

Road. Roy Tumelson and his sons were big rodeo people, and Roy himself was well known in rodeo circles as one of the best pickup men in the business. (Pickup men are the guys that take the cowboys off the bucking horses if they managed to stay on the horse until the buzzer sounded).

The Tumelson's were wise to our gang trying to sneak into their grape arbors and were always on the lookout for us. That was why it was so much fun to try to get some of their grapes. The Tumelson's back pasture bordered Lindsay Creek and the grapevines were between the house and the pasture. We had planned the raid for weeks, and we laid out an elaborate escape route down along the creek. If anyone spotted us and we had to run, we had paths and tunnels through blackberry thickets. We had made small holes in the wire fences that ran down onto the bank of the creek. They were just big enough for us small guys to get through, and the bigger people would have to go around.

One late evening, when it was barely light enough to see, four of us commenced the great grape raid! We successfully got to the grape arbors and were loading up with blue succulent grapes when one of the older Tumelson boys came out onto the back porch and saw one of us. He started shouting and cussing and hollered something about getting his shotgun. In a flash, we bolted and hit the escape route. The Tumelson boy was hot our heels trying to catch one of us. We all made it through the blackberry tunnels, but he avoided them by running up through the creek.

Now we came to the very small hole in the fence that he couldn't get through.

We had it made! My three partners in crime zipped through the small opening and I was the last to go through. Tumelson was only 10 yards behind. The last of my buddies through the opening must have loosened a single strand of bailing wire that sagged down across the opening. The combination of darkness and panic made it invisible to me. I had practiced diving through this hole successfully many times in our getaway rehearsals. I smiled to myself—I knew I had it made!

I was totally airborne with my arms outstretched, diving through the hole, when the wire made contact with the bridge of my nose, right between the eyes! My forward flight halted in midair and I crashed to the ground in front of the hole. In a flash, Tumelson had me by the back of my shirt. The bridge of my nose was pretty badly cut and I was crying because my nose hurt, but mostly because I thought Tumelson was going to kill me!

Tumelson was laughing hysterically and asked me if I was ok. He took me back to his house and he and his dad Roy, cleaned and bandaged my nose, which felt like it was a broken. Then they gave me a lecture and drove me home. When they let me out of their truck, Mr. Tumelson gave me a big bag of grapes and said if I wanted some more to just ask. He never told my dad that I had tried to steal his grapes. I guess he figured that the wire had been enough punishment. That was the day I acquired a huge admiration for the Tumelson's and lost my desire to steal grapes!

It snowed a lot in Lewiston one year and there was about two and a half feet of snow all over town. I was about 12 years old and I had gotten a flexible flier sled for Christmas. It was January and the temperature dropped well below zero—everything was frozen solid. Melted snow water turned to clear icicles hanging from the trees. The town looked like a display of ice carvings and the sled runs were icy and fast!

Mark Means Hill was only a few blocks from where we lived. They conducted professional motorcycle hill climbs there and the walking trails up the steep hill made great sled runs. When you got to the bottom of the hill you could coast for more than 100 yards. It was Saturday morning and all the kids from the neighborhood were sledding on the hill. Temperatures must have been around -20 degrees. The sled runs were icy and rough, but it was cool to just coast along smoothly for a long way when you hit the bottom of the hill.

On my last run, as my sled begin to slow to a stop, I stuck my tongue onto the metal plate at the front of the sled. I knew better than to do it, but there is an irresistible urge in kids to challenge common sense. I challenged, and I lost! My tongue locked onto the metal as if the world's greatest superglue bond had occurred. Now I had a 17-pound flexible flyer sled stuck to my flexible tongue!

There was no way I could let the other kids know what a stupid thing I had done, so I picked up the sled, carrying it straight up in front of me and started off for home. Some of the kids had just gotten to the bottom of the hill and shouted after me to ask where I was going. I wasn't going to turn around and let them see my tongue stuck to the sled so I just kept walking away, holding the sled up with one hand while quickly pointing toward home with the other.

When I got home, my tongue was hurting and I was almost in tears. My stepmother felt sorry for me, but couldn't control her laughter as she got some lukewarm water to help me get loose from the sled without tearing the skin off my tongue. So far I have successfully resisted subsequent urges to put my tongue on frozen metal, but who knows. If you ever see a news photo of an old man with a sled hanging from his tongue, it could be me!

As I moved through the gang stage years and became a new teenager, our activities got less mischievous and more dangerous. I remember crossing the Clearwater River at night by walking a single steel I beam when the Memorial Bridge was under construction. My favorite was playing in the railroad-switching yard. We would actually jump from the top of a boxcar of one train to the boxcar car of another while they were moving slowly.

There were huge sand piles along the tracks in the yard and we would jump off the boxcars onto the sand piles. It was about a 12 to 14 foot drop, and it was fun to do until one early December day. I was running along on top of the train cars with a friend of mine from across town who had never played in the train yard before.

"Watch this," I shouted as I hurled myself off the boxcar into the sand pile below. It was very cold that day and the sand pile was frozen solid. The impact rattled my teeth and knocked the wind out of me! As I rolled down the sand pile in pain and embarrassment, one thought entered my mind. Why should I be the only one? My friend was amazed to see me do that jump, and as his face appeared above the boxcar roof, I pointed and said, "It's a sand pile; jump, it's fun!" He complied almost immediately, proving that stupidity among kids is highly contagious. The look on his face as he impacted the frozen sand was priceless and even though I was still hurting from my jump, I broke up laughing! My friend was groaning and calling me names, but when we stopped hurting, we laughed about it. We weren't really hurt because we were still indestructible at that age.

They say cats have nine lives because they have a lot of close calls and still live. I think some people do too. I know I used up at least two of mine when I was a kid! There was a big water tower in the train yard. It was about 65 feet high and about 25 feet in diameter. The roof was shingled and it had a short spire sticking up in the center. It had a fairly steep, tapered roof. A wooden ladder ran from the ground to the roof. A set of cleats were nailed into the roof, and led from the ladder to the spire at the pinnacle. It was about 12 feet from the pinnacle to the edge of the roof. The shingles were old and covered with a slippery mold and moss. We would tie 15 foot ropes to the spire at the pinnacle and each one of us would hold onto a separate rope and chase each other around the roof playing tag. This is by far one of the more stupid things I let myself be talked into.

One day we were playing "Russian Roulette" roof tag on the water tower when my rope pulled loose from the spire. I was about 5 feet from the edge of the roof when I felt the rope go slack. I panicked, but my survival instinct made me drop to the roof flat onto my stomach with my arms outstretched toward the pinnacle. I slid down the roof about 18 inches and both of my feet dangled out over the edge of the roof. My fingernails dug into the moss covered shingles and I was frozen with the fear of falling.

Both my friends saw what a dangerous predicament I was in, and instead of immediately coming to my rescue, they taunted me, telling me I was slipping and today was that day I was going to die!! They were just doing stupid kids stuff, and would have felt horrible if I had really slipped off the roof before they tried to help me. It was just a cruel sadistic thing that kids sometimes do to each other.

I was too scared to move, or cry, or anything! I just laid there, clinging to life by my fingernails. After what seemed like an eternity, my friends retied my rope and passed it down to me. As soon as I got it firmly in my hands, I pulled my feet up over the edge and worked my way over to the ladder. Still scared and shaking, I climbed down and never went up there again! (That was life number one).

At age 14, I was riding in a car with some kids at the top of the Lewiston grade. The guy driving was speeding and passing cars. He lost control of the car on a sharp turn and we rolled end over end three times!

The driver was seriously injured, but lived. The other two kids my age had some cuts and lacerations—one had a broken leg. I suffered only torn ligaments in my right leg and a few bruises. (That was life number two) For several years after that crash, I felt very uncomfortable with speeds much over 40 miles an hour. In my pre-teen years, I came pretty close to fulfilling the legend of remaining in Shangri-La without aging!

CHAPTER 10

The Three Musty Ears

During my freshman year in high school I met my lifelong friends, Charlie Haag and Roy Clark. Charlie was a small wiry kid with a high-pitched voice that mellowed into a low voice before his senior year. Charlie was a good kid and a great friend. He lived across the river in North Lewiston on a small farm. The Haag's had cows, pigs, chickens, a huge vegetable garden, and some fruit trees. Charlie's mother was a small, wiry woman with a lot of energy. Charlie's dad was a big gentle man, who reminded me of Ben Cartwright on the Bonanza television series—he had many of the same mannerisms. I really liked Charlie's dad, and he seemed to like me.

Roy lived up in the Lewiston orchards on the south side of town, so our association was inner-city and multi-cultural. Roy played "B" squad football and Charlie was in the school band. All three of us joined the judo team. We got to be pretty good at throwing each other around and would put on demonstrations at the high school assemblies.

We acquired a new teacher at Lewiston senior high school who had been a gymnastics coach at Humboldt State College in California. His name was Sid Kinser, and he immediately formed an intramural gymnastics team at our school. Coach Kinzer seemed to like Charlie, Roy, and me. He learned that we were inseparable buddies, and he promptly named us "The Three Musty Ears." I'm still thankful our nickname never showed up in the "Bengal" (our high school annual). We never competed with any other schools in gymnastics, so consequently it was not a varsity sport in our school. We did provide halftime entertainment for our varsity basketball games. Roy, Charlie, and I performed on the flying rings. We were also on the high school archery team.

I have some unforgettable memories of our athletic endeavors during the halftime shows at our basketball games. The archery team was to put on a demonstration of sharp shooting. We shot swinging paper plates, the ace of spades off the end of a rotating wand, and extinguished a candle flame with one shot. They were mostly trick shots and could be done by any decent archer if they practiced and had good timing, but they were very impressive to the basketball fans, and we loved to perform!

In our archery show debut, I performed the final trick shot, which was to shoot a small balloon off the end of an arrow held by my buddy, Charlie. The shot was from 10 yards and was really no problem. The arrow that I was using was a target arrow, honed to a very sharp point, so it would pop the balloon and not just push it aside. The halftime show announcer explained the demonstration while I was busy organizing my equipment for the trick shot. I had my back to the target and I was supposed to whirl around, draw the bow, and shoot the balloon off the arrow with one smooth move. (Actually, you didn't shoot at the balloon, you shot at the center of the target where the balloon would be). A hush fell over the entire gym as I prepared to turn and shoot. To this day, after recalling the event with Charlie, neither of us knew what possessed him to do what he did. It was either blind trust, or dumb kid bravado!

When I whirled around to take the shot, Charlie had taken the balloon off the arrow and was holding it by the inflation stem between his thumb and forefinger! His right hand was only six inches from the main part of the balloon. The timing and the training I had rehearsed for the shot were automatic, and the arrow was already on its way to the target before I realized the danger of the situation. My heart was in my mouth during the short flight of the arrow. " Bang" went the balloon! "Thud" went my heart as it started beating again!

I stood there for several moments staring at the big smile on Charlie's face, his hand still clinging to the remains of the shattered balloon just a mere three to four inches from the arrow embedded in the center of the target. As fear drained from my brain, and my senses started functioning again, I could hear a great roar of applause from the crowd and Charlie took a bow.

Numbed by the experience, I just waved at the crowd. Then we picked up our show stuff and headed for the locker room. We were anticipating getting a severe dose of "what for" from our archery coach and any of the faculty that might have seen the halftime show. We were not disappointed. Oh well, no one was hurt; it was a heck of a stunt, and the crowd loved it, although they were never going to see it again!

Our gymnastics shows at halftime were not quite so risky, but there was an element of danger in our performance on the flying rings. The rings were sort of a trapeze act with two individual rings to hang onto, instead of a bar. At the peak of the swing on any given routine, the performer would be about 20 to 25 feet above the gymnastics floor. Below the length of the swing on the gym floor were tumbling mats laid end to end—not much to cushion a fall, but better than the hardwood floor!

We initially practiced with a tethered safety harness until we mastered the maneuvers, and then we did the routine without the tether. One of the maneuvers we were trying to master was the double cut. This is done when you reach the peak height on the backswing. You then bring both legs up over your arms. At the right moment you release both rings, so that your legs drop down passed your arms. The trick is to grab both rings again before the inertia separates you too far away to catch them. Failure to recapture the rings leaves the performer about 25 feet in the air with no rings, and no wings!

Neither Roy, Charlie, or I had ever perfected the double cut in practice, but we always had the safety harness on. After we would miss the rings and be dangling in midair, our safety harness line handlers would lower us slowly to the floor. Charlie was closest to mastering the "double cut". He was able to do it about every other time. Coach Kinser decided that we better not try it during the show.

At the next halftime show, Roy and I had finished our routines, which ended with some trick dismounts. (These were acrobatic ways of ending our performances and getting down from the rings). Charlie mounted the rings and began his act. After several maneuvers, he began to pump up his swing until he was reaching excessive heights for his normal routine. I was beginning to get a strange feeling for what might be coming, and I glanced over at Roy and the other two spotters, who were positioned under the backswing area. On the very next backswing apex, Charlie executed the Double Cut!!

The height was outstanding! The cut was spectacular, and the crowd fell silent with anticipation, but in spite of impeccable timing, both rings escaped Charlie by a fraction of an inch, and his hands clamped down onto "rings of the mind." Now, Charlie was suspended momentarily in midair, about 25 feet above the gym floor. I'm not sure what the crowd expected at this point, but Roy, the other spotters, and I knew what was about to happen.

The laws of gravity never fail, and Charlie started a long diagonal drop to the gym floor. Since his double cut attempt caught everyone by surprise, the spotters were really not in a good position to get to his impact point. The inertia of the high swing propelled him further out than we were expecting. We were about three feet short of getting into position to break his fall, and we all thought he was going to die. Charlie hit the end of the safety matt about four feet from the hardwood floor. He was still in a "tuck" position when he impacted the matt.

The compression on his body must have been horrendous, and how he was able to absorb the shock, I'll never understand. He was driven into the matt for brief moment on impact, and then he rebounded into a shoulder high back flip that landed him upright on his feet! The crowd roared, we were dumbfounded, and Charlie stood there on the end of the mat with his arm raised in a two-fisted pose as if the whole thing had been planned!

One by one, all the members of the gymnastic team began to applaud, and even our coach joined in the hand clapping, smiling, and shaking his head in disbelief! Coach Kinser would have some comments for Charlie when we got to the locker room. While Mr. Kinzer was simultaneously praising and chastising him, I mentally crossed off one of Charlie's nine lives!

My thoughts of Lewiston were interrupted periodically, as the dentists worked as a team, and had me open and close my mouth, while they fitted my new bridge. Finally at 2:15 a.m., I rose from the dental chair with a whole new set of front teeth. My mouth was still anesthetized, and I was groggy with fatigue, but from what I could see the bridge looked great! I gave my dentist and his friend big hugs and thanked both of them for helping me. We returned to the hotel, and I finally got to sleep around 3:00 a.m.

At 7:00 a.m., Susan, woke me with a gentle nudge and said, "Spence, it's time to get up. How do you feel?" Slowly, I swung my legs over the edge of the bed and sat for a moment. Other than sore muscles, stiffness in my legs, severe pain from the lacerations, and tenderness in my mouth, I felt great. "Can I go home now?" I said in jest. I put on my sweats, and we went down to the hotel restaurant for breakfast. I had oatmeal for breakfast that morning because chewing anything wasn't high on my list. I drank two cans of Nutriment after breakfast. I did some stretching exercises to loosen the stiffness in my body and I put off getting into the wetsuit until just before I had to get into the river.

We arrived at the Washington Water Power Dam about 8:15 a.m.; the crew had the jet boat waiting on the riverbank, just below the dam. After saying goodbye to everyone, I climbed into the boat, and put on the newly modified wetsuit. We had cut away the material and left holes where the suit had been chaffing the back of my legs and arms.

King backed the *No-Name* out into the turbulent water of the spillway and got me as close to the dam as possible with some margin of safety. We had to circumnavigate the dam this way. There was no boat lock for me to pass through, only a fish ladder, which I couldn't use.

I donned my fins, mask, and snorkel, and rolled off the boat into the churning white water at the base of the dam. I battled with the turbulence for about two minutes, and with four or five strong fin kicks, I propelled myself out of the white water and into the current heading downstream. The next stop was Wawawai, Washington about 35 miles down river.

It was about four miles from the dam to the Junction of the Clearwater and Snake Rivers and I would pass along the length of the city of Lewiston on the way. I saw groups of people waving from the banks and a few of my high school classmates held up signs from the class of 54 cheering me on. While swimming the stretch of river next to downtown Lewiston, I reminisced about my high school years, and my two best friends, Charlie and Roy.

CHAPTER 11

Lewiston Senior High

B y now Roy, Charlie, and I were like blood brothers. It was unusual to find one of us without the others. Our great loves were aviation and bow hunting, and we were generally engaged in one or the other. We were all heavily involved in Air Explorer Scouts. One year I won top honors at a regional Explorer Summer Camp at Geiger Air Force Base in Spokane, Washington. I got to ride in a T-33 jet trainer and fly over Lewiston. That did it! I was hooked on flight for life. The three of us were always hanging around the airport, hoping some pilot would take pity on us and give us a ride. Apparently we didn't look pitiful enough because no one ever did, but that didn't dampen our enthusiasm for flying.

During our senior year in high school the three of us had sixth period English Literature together. Our teacher was Maude Adams, known in our school as "Ma Adams." She was a heavyset, gruff lady with thick glasses, who looked over her spectacles at you when she was chastising you for something. Some kids did not like her, and some actually feared her, because of her stern countenance. I had her for one semester of US government and an English literature class. In spite of her gruff manner, I found her to be one of the best teachers I ever had, and I learned a lot from her. She had a poetry contest in her class one time and I won the contest with a poem about my buddy Charlie, and our unsuccessful bow hunts. After that, she seemed to like me a lot and tolerated some of my late assignments. Mrs. Adams, and Mr. Shinn both inspired and encouraged me to develop the potential they seemed to see in me.

During hunting season, Roy, Charlie, and I were chomping at the bit to go bow hunting for elk. By sixth period on fridays before the weekend hunts we were reduced to brainless bodies whose minds had already gone to elk country. We were useless as students, and Mrs. Adams knew it.

On the Friday before opening season we were sitting in class, fidgeting with anticipation. The car was packed with our hunting gear and supplies for the weekend, and we were agonizing at the 40 minutes still left on the large oak framed wall clock. Mrs. Adams was lecturing and writing on the blackboard (they were blackboards then). She had her back to the class, and without looking around she said, "I know that under normal circumstances, Spencer, Roy, and Charlie would be consuming this information with a scholarly appetite; but their minds have already transcended to their hunting camp. In order to protect my classroom clock from "staring damage", and because as students their concentration is no longer within their control, I am dismissing them early to get started on their hunt. Good luck, and this time, Charlie, get something!" The classroom erupted in hysterical laughter that faded from our ears as we sped down the school hall toward the door, out to our car, and the hunt! At that moment, all three of us loved "Ma Adams."

This was a very special time in our lives. We lived for bow hunting. We began salivating about two weeks before bow season and our minds could think of nothing else until we were loaded and on our way to camp! Roy, Charlie, and I practiced archery nearly all year round. We belonged to the local archery club and we practiced a lot at our club field range where you walked around trails, shooting targets at various distances. During our midsummer practices, we would do what we called "roving". We would hike around on hilly, open meadows and pick random targets. We would shoot at small bushes, dark spots on a dirt bank, or any target where we thought we wouldn't lose, or break an arrow.

Because we were still in our indestructible age, and our minds were not yet fully developed, we collectively came up with a hare-brained and dangerous game that required an equal amount of nerve and stupidity from each of us. We would space ourselves about 50 yards apart on separate knolls of an empty field. Using a broad-head arrow (a hunting arrow with a razor sharp point) one of us would lob the arrow high in the air on a trajectory that would drop it almost straight down on the spot where one of the other two stood on the opposing hill. When it landed, it was your turn to lob it at the next guy. Oh yeah, I forgot to mention that there was one rule. You could move only one of your feet when the arrow was descending on you. If you moved both feet to avoid becoming a shiskebob, you lost the game. The remaining two would continue until someone won.

Needless to say our practice sessions were creative and challenging, Having survived the practices, we were always ready for the hunt. In the years that the three of us hunted with the bow we had great adventures. If I'm able to remember them all, I'll have plenty of stories for my grandchildren.

The fall days were beautiful. They were cool and crisp in the early morning and pleasantly warm and sunny in the afternoon. We generally hunted the area around Deary and Boville, Idaho, small farm and saw-mill towns, about 70 miles from Lewiston This day we were somewhere around Moose Meadows. The landscape had pine, fir, and spruce woods, interspersed with various sized meadows. It was perfect bow hunting country.

The three of us were following a small herd of elk when we

came to a fast flowing creek, about 15 yards wide. It was too deep to wade across so we went downstream until we found a good size log bridging the stream. It was sturdy enough to hold our weight, but it was only about 10 inches in diameter. Crossing that log would be like walking a balance beam in gymnastics, but what the heck, we were gymnasts!

Charlie crossed first, using his bow as a balance staff. He wobbled once or twice, but crossed with no problem. I was next and had a nice smooth crossing. Roy was last and started out just fine. He paused for a moment, right in the middle of the creek, to steady his balance. It was then that the first yellow jacket wasp hit and stung him on the right ear. He yelled and grabbed his ear; the distraction almost made him lose his balance.

Charlie and I both focused on Roy where he stood perched on the log in the middle of the creek. The log was about four feet above the water, and he was keeping his balance. Charlie and I both saw the second yellow jacket as it headed straight for Roy's head. Zap! It got him on his ear within an eighth of an inch of the same spot as the first sting. This attack almost knocked Roy off the log, and he was starting to do a "soft-shoe pain dance", but he was hanging in there! Then Charlie and I stared in disbelief as no less than 20 or 30 yellow jackets came out of the nearby bush and headed straight for Roy's head. We yelled to warn him and he looked over a shoulder to see the swarm coming his way.

That was it for him. He pitched his bow in our direction, and then without hesitation, jumped into the swift moving creek. He was in midair when the lead yellow jacket scored a direct hit on the same ear within a quarter of an inch of the other two stings. Roy got in one more "ouch" before he momentarily disappeared beneath the surface. About 20 yards downstream, he scrambled out onto the bank and quickly checked to see if he had lost the yellow jackets. Charlie and I grabbed Roy's bow and high tailed it downstream before the critters acquired new targets.

We all joined up and moved far away from the battlefield. Roy's ear was swelling up and it was several times its normal size. He was soaking wet with this huge ear, and you know we had to laugh. Roy had survived the yellow jacket attack, and it was amazing that all three stings were almost in the same spot. Charlie wanted to draw a little bull's-eye target around the stings on Roy's ear.

Charlie and I loved Roy like a brother, but he was sort of a pariah when it came to hunting. Once, when I was in a hurry to get out of the car after a herd of elk crossed the road in front of us. My special forge-wood target arrows accidentally spilled out of my quiver and lay at an angle spanning the running board of the car to the ground. When Roy got out, he stepped on the forge-woods, breaking them in half. For a while I wasn't sure whether to hunt elk or Roy, but I forgave him because he felt as bad as I did; after all, he was my buddy. It probably made us even for the time I stuck him in the leg with a pitchfork.

One really cold fall day we went hunting at Cougar Meadows. We decided to camp right in the middle of the meadow where there was a small horse and cattle corral. We knew it was going to be below zero, so before it got dark we gathered enough firewood to make a big campfire and create enough coals to help keep us warm through the night. Roy's dad had bought him a new goose down sleeping bag that was supposed to keep you really warm, even in subzero temperatures. Charlie and I had second hand store specials made of cotton and something else. Roy was smug about his new goose down mummy bag, and reckoned Charlie and I would freeze while he was nice and toasty. Charlie and I laughed it off, but we had no idea how right he would be.

We built a huge fire and kept pretty warm until about ten o'clock when the temperature plummeted. The fire only did some good on one side so we kept turning in our bags, alternately warming and freezing both sides. Roy wouldn't shut up about how he was nice and warm all over in his new goose down mummy bag as Charlie and I slowly froze in ours.

We had a deal that we would take turns putting logs on the fire as long as we were awake, and it looked as if that might be pretty near all night for Charlie and me. When it was our turn, Charlie and I would scramble out of our sleeping bags in our shorts and T-shirts and quickly put a couple of logs on the fire, then scramble back to the semi-warmth of our bags.

Finally, it was Roy's turn to put wood on the fire, but rather than climb out of his warm bag he got the bright idea of getting to his feet with the mummy bag still zipped to the top. He would then bend down, pick up a log between his hands in the fold of the mummy bag, hop over and throw the log on the fire, all without ever leaving the warmth of his bag—brilliant! Now Charlie and I were even more envious of his bag.

It was on the last hop toward the fire, that he lost his balance. Roy, the log, and his bag all toppled into the fire! Roy was now trapped inside his mummy bag in the middle of the campfire. Charlie and I heard him holler as he fell and we were out of our bags in a flash! We both grabbed Roy's bag and drug him out of the fire. Thank God we got him out before he was seriously burned. He was lucky, and never even got singed. His bag however, was another matter. Fairly large holes were burned through the quilting cover and that exposed several areas of the goose down fill.

With the near catastrophe over, we stoked up the fire and returned to our bags to try and get some sleep. The wind started blowing around 2:00 a.m. and we got colder, and colder. Charlie and I were miserable most of the night, but took great satisfaction in knowing that Roy's once toasty bag was also getting colder and colder as the goose down spilled from the burnt patches and blew off into the frosty night. I loved hunting with Roy and Charlie—it was the highlight of my teen years!

To this day, I thank God that I grew up in northern Idaho and went to school at Lewiston Senior High. With few exceptions our student body was comprised of enthusiastic, disciplined kids with worthwhile goals. Even though we had the usual social cliques that develop in every high school, there was an exceptional code of fair play and ethics that was present in our school. Overt bullying of any student wasn't tolerated for long, and anyone playing the bully might find himself confronted by the school football team. There were no such things as gangs, except for a few kids with punk mentalities that hung around together outside of school. No one in our school ever faced the threat of being beaten, or killed, for their jacket or tennis shoes.

Those wonderful years ended all too soon. We woke up one morning and it was graduation time. We were typical high school seniors, elated to graduate, and anxious for the coming adventures of life. On graduation day we all sat and listened to the commencement address by our faculty and classmates, and then one by one we were called up to receive our diplomas.

It was a happy day and we all went out to dinner to celebrate. The next morning I was very surprised to see my picture in the Lewiston Morning Tribune. They had taken my picture as I was receiving my diploma and shaking the hand of the district official. Out of 156 seniors in the class of 1954, I don't know why they chose my picture for the paper. Charlie said it was because I looked happier to graduate than anyone else—maybe so!

CHAPTER 12

The Snake

My mental reverie about the high school days was shattered by the sight of a swarm of small green spheres and bright orange discs surrounding me in the water. They were so numerous that for a moment I thought I was asleep and in some psychedelic dream! I looked up from the water to see that I was floating in a sea of peas and sliced carrots! It was the discharge from one of Lewiston's large vegetable canneries. Three miles further downriver I was finally rid of the vegetables and I noticed a welcome rise in the water temperature. The Snake felt quite a bit warmer than the Clearwater. A few more miles down the Snake the water became disturbed, and the current was quite fast.

I was swimming on the east side of the river when I passed a large stretch of beach at a park where a number of people were swimming. Some of them waved to me and I waved back. Suddenly, a memory from my "east end kid days" hit me! This was the beach (Timothy Park, I believe) where a boyhood friend, Lloyd Cavanaugh, had drowned. Lloyd was only about thirteen years old. He and my friend Monte McMurray had been best friends. We were all part of the east end kids and we spent a lot of time together dreaming up innocent mischief to do.

All of us boys were good swimmers and it was a shock to our gang of kids when we learned that Lloyd had drowned. The current was definitely strong and the flow forced me away from the beach. I could see why Lloyd might have had a problem if he was fatigued or suffering from a cramp. For a couple more miles, I swam with the current, staring into the grey water that had claimed his life. I was trying to picture Lloyd's face. It was strange that I could picture everyone else's face, but not Lloyd's! After awhile the thoughts of Lloyd faded and the river took my full attention. Some back eddies and still areas made me pick up the work pace.

For some time the river paralleled the highway. Once in awhile fans would stop their cars, get out, and wave to us. I think they knew who we were because some of them held up signs. Unfortunately, they were too far away for us to read. After some time the river branched away from the highway and off into the rolling hills.

The rest of this second day was spent swimming through steep, sloping canyons on the backside of farm and ranch country. The river moved along steadily and for long stretches, there was nothing but water and river bank. By the afternoon, I had overcome most of the morning stiffness and was starting to season into the monotony and grind of steady swimming.

I took my noon meal in the water and stayed swimming in the river the entire day. At around 7:00 p.m. we arrived at Wawawai, a small settlement on a large bend of the Snake River. We were met at the dock by a small group of people who had come down from nearby farms to welcome us. While the boat docked, I swam to the beach alongside the dock and sat in the sand in shallow water. I didn't realize how tired I was until I stopped swimming.

I took off my fins, then stood up and waved to the small welcoming group. I walked slowly out of the water and the rolling motion was back again. I could feel the full effects of the combined two days and 83 miles of Clearwater and Snake Rivers.

I recognized two of the principals from EEE Corp among the people in the welcoming committee. After a few greetings from the town dignitaries and our hosts, the Snyder's, the EEE representatives asked to talk to me in private. I anticipated that they might have good news of more sponsors, but what they really came to tell me was that their manager had misrepresented the facts and that there were no sponsors! They also told me that they would not be able to honor their contract to sponsor me, and as far as EEE was concerned, the swim was off.

I was in shock! "You mean after 83 miles, you want me to quit?" Neither of the men looked at me; they just stared at the ground and shrugged their shoulders. "We can't afford the liability. Our Board convened an emergency meeting and voted not to support the swim any further." At first, a feeling of deep disappointment came over me; I couldn't think of anything except that all the planning, training and effort we had put into the swim so far would be lost in failure.

Slowly, the disappointment turned to frustration, and then to anger! In spite of being extremely fatigued, I thought I might find enough strength and energy to take both of the EEE men for a one-way river swim. "OK," I said, "If that's the way it is, it would be advisable for the two of you to get as far away from me as fast as possible!" Fortunately, the two men took my advice, got in their car, and left.

I watched as their car disappeared up the road, then I turned and walked back to the river. I was still in my wetsuit, so I walked into the water up to my waist and laid back, floating on the surface, just staring up at the evening sky. I laid there for some time, letting the cool waters of the Snake River cool my boiling blood.

The turn of events made me completely forget about my lacerations, which were still raw and irritated, and the soreness in my mouth from clamping down on the snorkel mouthpiece with my new bridgework.

After what seemed like a long time, I heard John and Bill calling to me from the dock. I lifted my head, and acknowledged them with a wave of my hand, then I stood up and waded to the beach. When I stepped out of the water, I told them the bad news. They stared in disbelief as I explained what had happened. "What now?" John said. "I don't know," I replied. "They're not supporting the swim, so as of now I don't think we have a safety boat anymore. Let's break the news to King Cole."

When I explained the situation to King, he lost it, and swore a big enough curse on EEE to make the one on King Tut's tomb sound like a blessing. "What will you do?" he asked me. "I don't know," I said. "I don't relish the idea of going on without the boat." He stood for a moment and said, "Let's go to the Snyder's home. I'll call Floyd Harvey, the owner, and see what he has to say."

It felt good to remove the damp wetsuit and get some warmth into my body and I threw on some sweats before we left the boat dock to go home with our hosts. The Snyder's were wonderful people and, they too, were outraged when we explained our new predicament.

When we got to the Snyder's home, King Cole called Floyd Harvey to explain what happened. King and Floyd talked for several minutes and then he handed the phone to me. "Floyd wants to talk to you," he said. Floyd's voice was firm, but warm and friendly. "I understand EEE backed out on us," he said. "I guess so," I answered. "If the boat and King stay with you, will you continue?" he asked. I thought for a moment, and then answered, "Yes sir. I told the world that I would make this swim and if the rivers can't stop me, I'm not going to be beaten by a corporation." There was a long pause, and then Floyd said, "Spence, as long as you are in the river pursuing your challenge, King and the boat will stay with you."

I thanked Floyd for his offer and support, but told him I had no idea how we would ever pay for the service. He said. "You just worry about the Snake and the Columbia, and I'll worry about getting paid." With that, he wished me luck on the rest of the swim and asked to talk to King again. They conversed for a few minutes and I heard King say, "Don't worry about me, Floyd. I'm staying until we make the Pacific Ocean."

King hung up the phone, and stared at me in silence. After a few minutes he said, "You need some food and rest. We have to make it to Central Ferry tomorrow." I nodded, and though I still felt resentment from the EEE deal, I started turning my anger into a resolve to complete the swim in spite of any circumstances.

After a great dinner with our hosts, we cleaned and dressed my wounds, and then went to bed. I didn't sleep very well that night, partly because of worry, but mostly because of pain and the persistent residual motion I could feel from swimming for hours in the rolling river.

At 6:00 a.m., the Snyder's gave us a wakeup call. After a good breakfast, we went down to the river. It was a beautiful morning with the rising sun already warming things up. There was a small crowd waiting at the landing to see us off. I dressed into my wetsuit, thanked the Snyder's for their hospitality, and thanked all the people who came down to give us support.

I waded into the water, put on my mask and fins and swam out into the middle of the river. It was the Fourth of July; we would celebrate my recent independence swimming to Central Ferry.

Sometimes while in an area of sparse population I would try to imagine what the river and the land bordering it must have looked like to Lewis and Clark. The barren hills rising up and bordering both sides of the river would have been devoid of any signs of civilization. Perhaps once in a while they may have seen a few Indian scouting parties up on the ridges, silhouetted against the blue sky.

Wild game should have been plentiful along the river but I understand that they fed mostly on salmon. They must have encountered miles of white water stretches, which have since been turned into lakes behind the dams.

It must have been a fascinating journey in a handmade canoe with an Indian princess for a guide, and I'm sure there were several days when portions of the Snake and Columbia Rivers were too rough and dangerous for travel by canoe.

CHAPTER 13

The Storm

Most of that third day was spent swimming in a steady flowing current with a few channels and some small rapids. Population along the river was sparse, mostly small farms and ranches. Throughout the day we would encounter small groups of people that waved at us as we passed by. When I swam into Central Ferry, about 6:30 p.m. that evening there was a huge group of people gathered at a Riverside Park. It was a big Fourth of July celebration for the area residents and they turned it into a welcoming party for our crew when we arrived.

Our hosts, Mr. and Mrs. Latham were there organizing the welcome. After swimming ashore and dressing out of my gear, I put on my sweats and went over to meet them. We joined the Fourth of July party for about two hours, had some great food and I visited with people in the crowd. They joked around with me asking if they could see my webbed feet, and did I think I would grow a set of gills by the time I reached the ocean? They were great people and they all wished me well.

One of the local reporters in the group told me that the Associated

Press and UPI had picked up the story and were reporting it nationally.

I gave him a story about swimming another 32 miles on the fourth of July. Finally, I succumbed to fatigue, and our hosts took us to their home where I quickly retired for the night. I rested a little better that night, but I could still feel the motion of the river.

Morning came early and the Latham's fed us a king's breakfast. By 7:30 a.m. I was back in the water again, headed for Riparia, which was about 30 miles down river. The day was overcast, and by noon it got very stormy, with strong wind gusts coming up the river. Because of the strong wind, I had to swim harder than usual and could not take much advantage of floating along with the current.

About 4:00 p.m., we were some miles upstream from Riparia, and approaching the upper Riparia rapids. The strong upriver winds had turned the Snake River into a violent seething mass of eight to ten foot waves. It was storming, with torrents of rain coming down. Wind spray lashed from the top of the waves with a force that stung the exposed parts of my face and head. I tried to keep my head submerged as much as possible, but I had to lift up often to try to get my bearings in the churning green water.

I was getting very concerned about going through the rapids in this storm. The water was getting violent and the visibility was so poor that I had no idea exactly where we were, and when we would reach the rapids.

After about an hour of swimming in large, miserable, breaking waves, I tried to talk to my boat crew. They were having their own time of it, trying to navigate the boat and stay in it. "Where are we?" I shouted as I got within a few yards of the boat. "We're not sure" came a reply that I could barely hear over the howling wind and thrashing water. "That's great." I returned. "Do you have any idea how close we are to the rapids?" "Pretty close I think," King shouted. "We can't see enough features on the shore to fix our position, but we should be very close."

Just a few minutes after my shouting match with the crew, I

slid into a trough and actually saw the bottom of the river. Next, I banged into a huge boulder and got sucked underwater for a few seconds. When I finally got to the surface and rode up on to the crest of a wave, I shouted at the boat which was dangerously close to me. "I just hit a big rock, so I guess you're right! You guys keep sharp, it's about to get real dangerous out here!"

That was the last contact I had with the crew for the next thirty minutes. Every time I submerged into a trough, I either saw big rocks or hit them. During one encounter, I passed between two huge boulders and got sucked around behind one of them. I was trapped there in the "suck hole" until I broke free by pulling myself up the rock. I had to hold my breath long enough that when I finally made it to the surface, I was pretty sure that trees on the shore bent toward me when I took my first breath! Now I was getting pulled into trough after trough, and every time I went down I could see the bottom of the river. I kept very busy fending off big rocks as they appeared, and once in a while I would have to try for a breath-holding record. Suddenly there was a really big boulder right in front of me and I was forced over it and up to the surface. When I rode to the crest of the wave I took a quick look around for the boat and my crew. They were nowhere in sight!

After several more tours of the river bottom, and some head on encounters with big rocks, I could no longer see the bottom and I seemed to be out of shallow water. I was mostly on the surface, getting beat up again by the wind and waves.

Visibility had decreased significantly because of the rain, wind, and spray, and it was difficult to see anything, even from the crest of the waves. I had no idea where the boat crew was, and I tried to find them each time I rode up on top of a wave. I was worried that something had happened to them. I could ride these huge waves, but the crew could be having big trouble with the boat. I knew King was a good rough water boat handler in wild rapids, but these huge waves with short distances between the crests were a different matter.

The wind got stronger and stronger, and the surface of the river took on the appearance of competition surfing waves. I was having trouble seeing where I was in the river, and I had no idea what lie ahead downstream. I couldn't find the boat, and now I could barely see the banks of the river. After another mile or two of fighting the water and looking for the boat, it finally appeared when I rode up on top of a huge wave. The boat was about 30 yards away on top of another wave. I shouted as loud as I could to get the attention of the crew. Fortunately, they saw me but it took about 20 minutes before they were able to safely work their way over to me.

I told King that we had better get out of the middle of the river before we had a major problem. Even though we were only about two miles from Riparia, I said we should quit for the day and start from the same point tomorrow. I boarded the jet boat and we made our way to the Riparia side of the river. There we got some relief from the tremendous pounding we were taking in mid-river. We were amazed at how rough it could get on this stretch of the Snake. The relentless upriver winds blasting against the fast-moving current turned the river into a marine monster that roared and lashed out at anything that floated.

Finally we got down river to the Riparia landing. Our host, Bill Evans, and some people were there watching for us from inside their cars and trucks, trying to avoid the wind and rain. They couldn't believe we actually made it with the river as rough as it was. They helped us secure the boat behind the dock to protect it from the rough water. We climbed into Bill's station wagon and he took us to his home for supper and a much-needed rest. After five hours of battling the stormy river we were all dead tired.

That night I remember saying a prayer, and asking for the storm to be over by morning. I had no desire to try to swim through the notorious Texas, and Palouse Rapids, and then take on the Lyons Ferry whirlpools under the conditions that we faced today. I turned out the light and closed my eyes. The rolling motion was worse that night, and I dreamt about fighting the river waves. I took some consolation in the fact that we covered 30 more miles, but those last five hours made us pay. It was a restless night for the crew and me.

River Swimmer Slowed By 10-Foot High Snake Waves

RIPARIA — "I'm beginning to feel like a fish," marathon swimmer Spencer Campbell remarked Thursday after battling 10-foot high waves in a 17-mile leg of his swim to the Pacific Ocean from Orofino.

Campbell was a fish out of water for all but four hours in his third day of a 557-mile trip, calling a halt at 3 p.m. near this Snake River community.

"It was a rough day," the former deep sea diver said. "The winds were blowing at 20 miles per hour and there was a lot of dust. But I feel good and ready to go at it again."

'Went Through Them'

Asked how he contended with the high waves, the confident Orofino resident said "I didn't have much choice, I just went right through them."

After his dip in water he described as "abnormally cold" for this time of year, Campbell went ashore at the Bill Evans ranch where he looked forward to "10 hours of rest and a good meal."

Campbell predicted he would reach the headwaters of the Ice Harbor Dam pool by Friday evening. This is a 30-mile swim from Riparia to Kahlotus.

If this schedule is maintained, Saturday Campbell hopes to make another 30 miles "in calmer water where I'm going to have to do some hard swimming," and reach Ice Harbor Dam.

Once there, he will feel even more like a fish. Dam officials have agreed to let him descend the fish ladder. Campbell said he understands a reception is planned at Ice Harbor.

"If everything works out, I'll be at Pasco early next week," said the plucky Campbell, adding, "This is a terrific way to see some beautiful country."

Campbell had a word of praise for the crew manning the boat that precedes him each day of the trip. "I couldn't ever make it without them. They are a real team."

One of the reasons only 17 miles were charted Thursday—the fewest so far—was because the boat had trouble navigating in the rough water, Campbell said.

Sticks With Forecast

Despite the trouble, the 25-year-old Campbell is sticking with his 30-day prediction for reaching Astoria, Ore., by way of the Clearwater, Snake and Columbia rivers.

Since his start Monday, he has traveled 126 miles. There are 431 miles remaining. The distances covered have shortened each day since the start, when he made 45 miles from Orofino to the Washington Water Power Co. dam east of Lewiston. Tuesday he made 34 miles and Wednesday 30 miles.

CHAPTER 14

~~~~~~~~
~~~~~~~~

Rapids and Whirlpools

At 7:00 a.m., we were back on the river. The storm had passed in the night. The sun was up, there were blue skies and the marine monster we escaped from yesterday looked like a river again. King ran the boat about three miles back up stream, and I dropped into the water.

There was a moderate current, and the water actually felt restful when not having to fight any waves. When we approached the Riparia railroad bridge we passed the landing where Bill Evans and the small group of fans waited to wave at us and send us off. I waved to them from the river, then we turned toward the day's goal of reaching "Wind Dust" and the challenge we would face getting there.

About three miles downstream from the bridge was the Snake River trilogy, the Texas rapids, the Palouse rapids and the whirlpools of Lyons Ferry, but now there was just the gentle massage of the water. My mind wandered off to thoughts of my childhood and San Francisco. Suddenly, I was aware of loud shouts from my brother Bill. "Spence! Spence!" I raised my head reluctantly from my floating rest and I saw Bill and John pointing downriver. They looked very excited and I knew that the bell had sounded for our next round with the Snake.

At first the river picked up speed, and after a few minutes I could hear the roar of the rapids coming from downstream. When we got to the start of the wild water, I was paying strict attention! I tried to coordinate with my crew to find out which side of the river I should take to minimize the risk. Unfortunately, there wasn't enough time for any such strategy. The crew was too busy figuring out where they were going to go to avoid disaster, so I was on my own. After only a few minutes into the headwaters of the rapids, it became painfully obvious to me that if there was a safe channel through the rapids, I wasn't in it!

The first major area of challenge was a fast water chute, which ricocheted my body off some very jagged boulders. They were sharp enough to tear my wetsuit and cut my shoulders and legs. Then, an area of suck-holes pulled me underwater and held me there until I pulled myself laterally along a submerged rock wall far enough to escape the undertow. On the surface again, I found myself sailing through a torrent of whitewater with my back pointing downstream. This was not good!

It's extremely dangerous to go through violent rapids backwards where you can't see what's coming. I struggled to get turned around, but it was too late! The irresistible force of the raging water blasted me across a large shallow rock, and literally tossed me into the air for a few yards. I landed against another huge rock, which momentarily knocked the wind out of me. I was in serious trouble. Trying to catch my breath, I abandoned the snorkel tube to get some unrestricted air, then, I accidentally breathed in some water. Now I almost panicked!

Miraculously, I had entered a fairly deep channel of slower current and the surface smoothed out for a distance of about 50 yards. There was just enough time for me to jettison the light weight-belt around my waist, cough up some water, and get a few desperate breaths of air. I barely had my breathing somewhat under control and my snorkel back in my mouth, when some white water and suck-holes pulled me under again. Now I was squeezed through a narrow channel between two large boulders. Again, I could feel the suit, and some of my flesh being torn by the rocks!

The Texas rapids was about one and a half miles long, and I had probably only passed through the first half-mile. I could not see the boat or the crew and I had no time to look for them. I was far too focused on my survival! For the next half-mile it was more of the same.

At times I was held underwater until I thought my lungs would burst. It seemed as if the suck-holes were getting stronger, or I was getting weaker.

Finally, after what seemed like an eternity, I found myself in some deep, slow moving water at the end of the Texas rapids. It was there that I finally caught up with the boat and crew. John shouted to ask me if I was OK, and I shouted back that I had taken on some serious pain. All I could do during the three and a half miles to the start of the Palouse rapids was to rest and pray that they weren't as bad as the ones I just came through.

The recuperation period was not nearly long enough and John called to me as he raised his arm and pointed downstream. "Looks like a real rough spot coming up in about 70 yards!" "Oh goodie, I can hardly wait!" I shouted.

The first few hundred yards of the "real rough spot" was aptly described. Besides the beating I was getting on the rocks, I could see blood, lots of it, coming from somewhere. It was somewhat unnerving to know that the somewhere was my body. At several points, I was totally out of control, like a small rag doll being flushed down a toilet. The buoyancy and chaffing protection of the wetsuit was the main reason I wasn't drowned or seriously injured.

The last half-mile of rapids slowed down considerably and the river turned from a churning, whitewater torrent into a long, peaceful, fast moving stream. The boat crew came alongside in the quiet water to check on my condition. My brother, Bill, leaned over the side of the boat to talk with me and immediately noticed the blood. "You're bleeding pretty bad," he said. "Where are you hurt?" "What part of my body do you want me to start with?" I quipped. "I'm not sure exactly where I'm bleeding, but there's enough of it to worry me," I said. I drifted along with the boat for a few hundred yards, resting and trying to assess the damage. The swimming day was only a couple of hours old, and I was not looking forward to the rest of it!

The tranquility of my short rest period was shattered when John announced loudly that we were coming into the Lyons Ferry Whirlpool area. There was no time now to lick any wounds. We knew that this area could be tough to swim through because of the violent mixing of waters where the Palouse River merges with the Snake. Here, we expected to find a lot of very disturbed water with huge boils and whirlpools that could suddenly appear and grow large enough to cause a problem.

When we rounded the last bend before Lyons Ferry, the river widened. The Palouse River would join us on our right. John was studying the area downriver, and finally turned and shouted in my direction. "Rough water is coming up in about 300 yards but it doesn't look too bad." That was the first encouraging news I had heard since, "It's a beautiful morning." Maybe the Lyons Ferry Whirlpool area was more mariner tall tales than fact—I could only hope.

Soon we were in an expanse of roiling and boiling water, and I could feel strange undercurrents tugging at my legs. I had to struggle around three or four back eddy current areas, but nothing as bad as I had anticipated. We moved out into the main confluence of river with the most turbulent water. I was sailing along in the current, occasionally swimming through huge boils that welled up from below.

I was beginning to get comfortable when my brother Bill shouted from the boat, "There's a huge whirlpool starting about 40 yards ahead." Before I had time to switch from my momentary complacency to an alert mode, the *No-Name* swerved to the right and left me staring into, and heading right for, a huge sucking whirlpool which appeared to have a vortex about ten feet deep. At that moment I became envious of Lewis and Clark's canoe!

I immediately tried to swim off to one side, but the swirling perimeter current caught me and started pulling me around the edge of the gaping hole. I cast a few quick glances down into the vortex and didn't like what I saw. I was afraid to get pulled into the hole, not knowing what would happen after that. I started swimming as hard as I could to keep from being sucked down into the vortex. Suddenly, the whirlpool made a weird groaning sound and began to fill up with water, converting it into a huge boil, which pushed me away from its center and sent me out into the main downriver current.

I later learned that King Cole, seeing that I was in danger of getting pulled into the vortex, drove the *No-Name* quickly upstream and turned the boat so that the discharge of water from the jet engine would shoot out into the center of the whirlpool. Apparently the addition of water forced into the vortex disturbed the mechanics of the whirlpool and helped to destroy it. King said he learned about the whirlpool killer thing from his Hell's Canyon experience. I wasn't sure if that's what really killed the whirlpool, but I silently thanked both God and King Cole for their help.

About two miles downstream from Lyons Ferry we had another exciting event when my brother-in law, John, narrowly avoided swimming between two huge concrete bridge supports that had a hidden log jam between them. John had jumped into the river to swim with me, and I was about 40 yards ahead of him when I passed the structures and saw the log jam almost hidden beneath the surface.

I looked upstream and saw him swimming toward the opening, fully intending to go between the two piers. I yelled as loud as

I could, and frantically motioned for him to swim wide of the two supports. He got the message, but almost too late, and actually hit one of the supports before he was able to pull himself around to the outside of the concrete pier. John told me later that he almost couldn't keep from going between them! If that had happened he would have been sucked down, impaled against the log jam, and drowned. The score was now: us two, Grim Reaper: zero, and we were trying to keep it that way.

Two or three miles below the bridge we went ashore to assess the damage I had sustained in the rapids. I was still bleeding from several places and the wetsuit was sliced open at those sites. I had three pretty deep lacerations and three more severe abrasions, all of which were still bleeding. One deep laceration looked as if it might require stitches.

Our first aid kit wasn't equipped for anything too severe. The best we could do was to clean the wounds with some sterile water and coat them with petroleum jelly. We then bound wetsuit material against the injured areas with strips of gauze. After our first aid session we returned to the river and started the downstream swim again. The river ran through some hillside areas and then along ranch country. Once in awhile we would see people working who seemed to recognize us and would wave to us from their trucks and tractors.

That day's 28-mile swim seemed longer than expected, and it was about 6:00 p.m. when we arrived at Windust to meet our welcoming party, led by Mr. and Mrs. Shautz from Kalotus, Washington. They were very concerned about my injuries and wanted to take me to a doctor. I deferred, saying I thought the bleeding had stopped and we would check the wounds when we got to their home. I just didn't want any negative medical opinions tempting me to quit the swim.

Later at their home we found the wounds had stopped bleeding and we cleaned and dressed them in sterile bandages. I was bruised in several places, and had aches and pains everywhere, but I was alive and about 173 miles closer to the Pacific Ocean. I was too tired to be restless in spite of the motion, and for the first time on the swim I actually got some good sleep.

Whirlpool Spins Swimmer Until Boatman Breaks Water

KAHLOTUS — "I'll never swim that stretch of water again," river-wise Spencer Campbell vowed Friday after nearly being drowned in a whirlpool at Lyons Ferry.

"I've never experienced anything like it," he said after emerging from the Snake River after eight hours, which put him within 399 miles of his goal to swim from Orofino to the Pacific Ocean and Astoria, Ore. Campbell covered 32 miles Friday.

"I got sucked into the whirlpool about two hours after we left Riparia. I couldn't get out. Then my two safety divers came to rescue me and they couldn't get out. It looked bad.

"But the boat driver (King Cole of Spokane) drove the boat through the whirlpool and broke it up enough so we could get out."

Water Turbulent

Once past Lyons Ferry at the confluence of the Snake, Tucannon and Palouse rivers, Campbell found the going easier although there was "a lot of turbulence."

In fact, several hours before this self-styled fish flopped ashore at 5 p.m. he was in the slack-water of the Ice Harbor Dam pool and had to do most of the work to make any progress.

After devouring a steak at the P. A. Shautz trailer camp at Kahlotus, Campbell, with Cole and his safety divers, Bill Campbell and John Craig, huddled for a strategy meeting and evolved a new plan.

"Saturday," Campbell explained, "the winds on the Snake River are supposed to blow upstream from five to 15 miles per hour.

"So, we decided to do the swimming at night. I plan to go into the water about 6 p.m. and swim all night, arriving at Ice Harbor (28 miles) sometime Sunday morning."

Campbell, in finishing his swim Friday, had completed five days in the water and has traveled 158 miles. After flipping down the Ice Harbor fish ladder he expects calm water the rest of the way to Pasco, where he plans to arrive early next week.

"I feel fine," the 25-year-old former deep-sea diver said here as he rested. "This trip seems to agree with me. I'm up to 148 pounds after hitting a low of 144 pounds.

"But I wouldn't give a plug nickel for a swimmer's life in those rapids and whirlpools at Lyons Ferry."

CHAPTER 15

Ice Harbor Dam

The next day our target was the Ice Harbor Dam, 30 miles downriver. Around 2:00 p.m. the winds got very bad, and we suspended swimming until they died down around 6:00 p.m. Even though there were additional risks involved, we elected to swim at night to avoid the winds. I swam in the dark, navigating my way by keeping the *No-Name* off to my side about three feet away. It was difficult for the crew to navigate their way down the river in the dark, and at times we had stop to make sure we were following safe channels.

It was a strange feeling swimming in the dark, staring into the black water. At 3:00 a.m., we could see the lights of Ice Harbor Dam about two miles ahead and we decided not to approach any closer in the dark because there was no preventive barrier other than a line of warning buoys to keep a boat from reaching the edge where the water spills over the dam. I wasn't about to add a 100-foot plunge over the spillway to my growing repertoire of river experiences.

We located a boat dock in the reservoir park they called the Levey. We found the park restroom and went in to get out of the wind chill coming off the river. I probably should have taken off the damp wet suit, but I was so tired I just lay down next to the sink and urinal and took about 45 minutes of semi sleep sprawled out on the concrete floor. At 5:00 a.m. a fisherman came in to use the bathroom and got a real surprise when he found the whole crew sleeping on the bathroom floor.

I got up and went outside into the morning sunrise. There was no one to assist us and we had no idea how to proceed from this point. We knew that we had to go through the locks at Ice Harbor Dam, but we had no contact with anyone to let us know the lock schedule, or what to expect at the Tri Cities. There was also no way to contact anyone from the park.

Things were looking pretty bleak when a man who was camping with his kids talked with us and offered to take one of us into town to make a call to get some assistance. I got elected, since I was the only one who could make a collect call and get connected. I jumped into the back of their camper and sat next to two little kids, one girl about eleven and a boy of eight or nine. They regarded my raggedy, wet suit clad appearance with some apprehension, but were quite charitable about sharing their seats with me.

Their father was taking them to Mass, and then they were going to return to the reservoir to finish their camping trip with a day of boating. They asked me why I was in a wet suit and why I looked so tired. When I told them I had been swimming all night, they looked at each other, shrugged their shoulders and didn't say another word the rest of the way into town. I was way too tired to explain, so I just let my head bang against the jogging camper wall, and tried to grab some sleep.

They let me off at a service station where there was a pay phone. It took a couple of calls to the media and they were able to locate what was left of our support crew. After waiting by the phone booth for about 15 minutes, I got a call from Dave Sinclair, the manager of the Orofino radio station. When EEE had abandoned the swim he offered to assist us with some help and sponsorship for the rest of the trip. He told me they had arranged for Media and Water Follies dignitaries from the Tri Cities to meet us with a big cabin cruiser at the bridge where the Snake River flows into the Columbia. In order to make the 9:00 a.m. rendezvous I would have to swim to the Ice Harbor Dam and go through the locks with the morning boat traffic.

Dave picked me up from the service station and drove me back to the levy. After some briefing of the boat crew, we were ready to start the swim into the Tri Cities. It was a short swim from the park to the boat locks at Ice Harbor Dam. When we reached the boat locks we had about a twenty-minute wait for the locks to open. Lying there in the water with my head submerged, I could hear familiar underwater sounds coming from the dam. Resting and listening to the pulsating sounds took my thoughts back to Jack London Square.

During my last year in the Air Force I became the Training Director for our base Underwater Recovery Team. I vacillated between staying in the Air Force and becoming a pilot, or pursuing a career in deep sea diving. Although flying was my first love, and I wanted to stay in the Air Force for a military flying career, I had a strong fascination with diving and was equally taken with the idea of becoming a deep sea diver.

It was December 1, 1958, about 4:30 in the afternoon. I had just finished conducting a training dive at our crash boat dock in Mukilteo, a small township on the Puget Sound about three miles north of the base.

I had already dressed out of my diving gear into warm clothes and was sitting on a driftwood log which had washed up on the beach alongside the dock. I was watching a couple of my team divers who were finishing up their diving exercises and trying to ignore the cold. I was reading *Skin Diver* magazine. There was an interesting article on the "Coastal School of Deep Sea Diving" in Oakland, California, and there were great pictures of divers in Navy Mark

Five deep sea diving gear.

The article highlighted the glamorous and adventurous nature of deep sea diving and pointed out that with the right underwater jobs, a commercial diver could make good money. Just the adventure and mysterious nature of the underwater world presented an irresistible challenge to me, so on that day sitting on a log by the sea, I cast the die and it came up "diving."

My enlistment was up on December 11th and I had only 10 days to clear the base muster out and become a civilian again. The first week or two off the base felt very strange, and I thought that the guys who do 20 or 30 years in the service must have to do some real adjusting. My adjustment didn't take too long and I got busy planning to go to Deep Sea Diving School.

There was a new class starting in February, so there would be time to visit with Susan, and friends and family before I had to leave for Oakland. I had met Susan several months before at a party in Clarkston while on a weekend pass and we were dating at the time. I spent most of the two months visiting with my dad and spending time with Susan and her folks. During that time, Susan and I had a great courtship. Susan's father, Doc Craig, and her mother, Jean, were very supportive of our relationship. I also spent a lot of time reading everything I could get my hands on about diving and had daydreams about the adventures that life as a diver would bring. Little did I know what kind of excitement was in store for me!

About one month before I was to leave for diving school, I was reading an article in *Skin Diver* magazine written by master diver, E.R. Cross. The television program, "Sea Hunt," starring Lloyd Bridges was very popular at that time and there was some speculation that the lead character of the series, Mike Nelson, was inspired by E.R. Cross. Mr. Cross lived in Hawaii and the article contained his address so readers could submit comments and information for his *Technifacts* column.

One Sunday evening an inspirational whim came over me and I

picked up the phone and called Hawaii information to see if I could get E.R. Cross's phone number—no problem. Now that I had the number, did I have the nerve to call him and what would I say? "I want to be a deep sea diver. Can you give me some advice?" That would sound rather presumptuous I thought. After some procrastination, I dialed the number.

The phone rang several times, and I was about to hang up, somewhat relieved, when the receiver clicked and a distinctive voice said, "This is Cross." After a moment of hesitation, I said, "Mr. Cross, you don't know me. My name is Spence Campbell. I live in Spokane, Washington. I'm 22 years old. I just got discharged from the Air Force and I'm registered for the deep sea diving class starting in February at the Coastal School in Oakland. I'm a great admirer of yours, and I wonder if you would be willing to give me some advice."

There was a moment of silence from his end, and then he said in his warm, friendly tone, "Sure, for what it's worth, I'd be happy to answer any questions you might have—shoot." For the next 20 minutes or so two things happened. First, I learned that ER Cross was a wonderful, giving person who answered all my questions.

He told me that my chosen path would not be easy, and not to expect any more from the diving profession than I was willing to put into it. He was very candid about the pitfalls inherent in deep sea diving as a profession, but he said if my heart and my mind were set on it, and I was willing to sacrifice to succeed, then to go for it and give it everything I had. The other thing that happened in that 20 minute phone call was the start of a lifetime relationship between E.R. Cross and me. He became my inspiration, personal friend, and mentor throughout my diving career.

CHAPTER 16

Deep Sea Diving School

I packed some clothes and books, said my good-byes, and boarded a bus for Oakland. My mother, my brother Alan, and his wife Bunny lived in Redwood City. They met me at the bus station in Oakland when I arrived. I visited with them for a couple of days, and then my sister, Jean, who lived in Stockton drove down to visit with us and took me over to Oakland to get me situated.

I rented a room at a small hotel, about three blocks from the diving school. It was actually a boarding house which catered to students from the diving school. In addition to our room, we would get two meals and a sack lunch each day, except for Saturday. The people who owned the hotel were Seventh-day Adventists and did not serve meals on Saturday.

I had one great meal at a nice waterfront restaurant, courtesy of my sister. Then she dropped me off at the hotel and went back to Stockton.

During the next two days before class started I met several of my classmates. There would be about 16 of us in the February class and ten of us were staying at the hotel.

Three guys from the last graduating class were still at the hotel and would be leaving in a couple of days. We all got together to get acquainted, and the graduates filled us new students full of B.S. about the course. They told us we would have to make a night dive in the estuary after they chummed for big sharks. They said one of the exercises was to take a water jet—dig a big hole in the soft bottom until you were completely buried under 10 feet of mud. Next, they would shut off the jet and leave you trapped there for a long time in the dark under the mud—until they turned on the jet and let you dig yourself out. We knew some of the stories were meant to hassle us, but we didn't know how close to the truth the water jet experience would be.

Some of the students and I took a walk down to Jack London Square on the Sunday before class started. The diving school was located on the Oakland estuary next to an upper class seafood restaurant named The Sea Wolf. The school was closed for the weekend but from what we could see, it consisted of a group of blue and white buildings situated on a long wooden dock. Next to the school dock, we could see a barge-like platform about 40 feet long and 20 feet wide. It had four metal laders leading from the deck of the platform down into the water and we commented about how we would all soon be climbing up and down those ladders in heavy deep-sea diving gear.

On the east side of the school dock and diving platform there was a big area of open water terminating at a large wharf. Moored alonside that wharf was an historical old sailing ship the "Sea Wolf". It was once owned by the famous author Jack London and was the subject of one of his books. The wharf had shops with nautical memorabilia and for a nominal fee, you could get a tour of the sailing ship, it was a local tourist attraction: thus the name "Jack London Square". The sights and sounds of the square made you feel nautical.

The spring air was damp and smelled of low tide. Some seagulls flew overhead, while others occupied various perches on railings and pilings. Their cries, along with the wind and lapping water against the shore and docks, and the occasional distant sound of a ship's horn out in the bay, performed a natural waterfront symphony. The marine environment was stimulating and it sparked a feeling of excitement and anticipation in all of us.

Back at the hotel my new classmates and I hung out and talked about our upcoming adventure. The weekend passed quickly, and on Monday morning after a family-style breakfast, all the new diving students walked the three blocks to the waterfront together.

The school was open and a dark-haired young lady greeted us as we entered the reception area. She moved among us, handing each one of us a notebook with our name on it, and continued registering and handing out notebooks until all the students had arrived. She then led us down a hall through a large storage room filled with all kinds of diving equipment and into a small classroom that could accommodate about 20 people. We all took seats at the schoolroom style desks. On each desk was a thick, blue book titled, *Submarine Medicine Practice.*

About five minutes after we sat down a short, stocky man with a cocky swagger, entered the classroom wearing a tan uniform with diving helmet pins on his shirt lapels. It was Al Mikalow, owner of the Coastal School of Deep Sea Diving. I recognized him from the school brochures and articles in *Skin Diver* Magazine. Al was a flamboyant character, with a good sense of humor, but at times he could be a bit tyrannical! He gave us his patented welcoming speech, and we all got the distinct impression that the training and discipline would be patterned after the U.S. Navy Deep Sea Diving School. He then introduced our class instructor, Master Diver Eugene Mogus, U.S. Navy Ret. We knew for sure that the training would subscribe to the three D's, Disciplined, Demanding and Difficult.

After briefing us on the rules and regulations of the school, Mr. Mogus took us on a tour of the school facility, then he released us for lunch. He told us all to report to the equipment room at 12:30

p.m. The lunch break gave us a chance to meet some more of our classmates. There were several characters in our class. One student was a tall, thin, dark-haired young man from Houston, with a heavy Southern drawl. We promptly name him, "Tex". Tex had a great sense of humor and was always wisecracking. He had an affinity for black leather clothes. His jacket, hat, and boots—everything was black!

There was a tall, distinguished looking German gentlemen, about 48 years old with piercing blue eyes and a direct, bordering on arrogant demeanor. Hans Jastrom was the owner of a marine service company in Caracas, Venezuela. He told us he had been a submarine command officer in the German Navy. He was a real seaman, and once he warmed up to us, he shared a lot of his knowledge and experiences. He became a good friend.

Glenn Lewis was a sturdy built, tall man in his late thirties. He was retired from the Navy after 20 years and had been a member of the U.S. Navy underwater demolition team.

Richard (Dick) Spear had been a sport scuba diving instructor for Mel Fisher's Dive Shop in Redondo Beach, California. This was the same Mel Fisher who is now famous for all the gold and silver treasure recovered from the Spanish ship, "Atocha."

Dick had trained a number of movie stars and famous people to scuba dive. Just before coming to the school he had trained Henry Mancini and his family. Dick was very sharp, with a great sense of humor. He became a real close friend.

John Hardaway was a young man who was tired of college and training to become an accountant. He wanted a career with adventure and came to deep sea diving school to see if he could find what he was looking for. John was a hard worker and a good friend.

We all assembled in the equipment room after lunch and were divided into teams by colors. I was assigned to the white team with three others: Dick Spear, John Hardaway and Glenn Lewis. Because of Glenn's Navy diving experience, he was named team leader and would be responsible for the team diving and tending schedule, and ensuring that all divers in the team accomplished their duty assignments and class projects.

There were four teams: White, Red, Blue, and Green. Each team had four students. After the team assignments, each team was issued a Mark Five Navy Diving Helmet and Breastplate weighing 54 pounds, four rubberized canvas diving suits, each weighing about 22 lbs, 200 feet of lifeline and air hose, two 18 pound lead/canvas shoes, and an 84 pound lead weight belt. All totaled, when dressed and standing in full Mark Five diving gear, the diver would be supporting approximately 194 pounds of equipment.

Our first practical training assignment was to learn to strip down, clean, and do maintenance on the diving equipment. Diving dresses had to be patched and tested; the lifeline and air hose also had to be checked and re-taped. During the first week it was classroom theory in the mornings and equipment orientation and maintenance training in the afternoons.

Toward the end of the first week we were studying diving physics and physiology and learning how to dress each other into heavy Mark Five diving gear. We worked as a team with two of us dressing the diver and one man controlling the divers air supply and communications. At first we were only allowed to dress into the gear. We would stand up and take a few steps toward the diving ladder, then turn around and walk back to the bench. We then sat down to be undressed by the tenders. When we were not practicing dressing in the diver, we were cleaning and polishing our diving gear.

To get a picture of how this diving gear works, first, the diver puts on a large rubberized canvas suit, then a brass breastplate fits over the head of the diver and rests on his shoulders. A rubber gasket built into the collar of the suit provides a watertight seal between the dress and the breastplate. The gasket is rimmed with holes which fit over brass bolts projecting from the breastplate. The gasket is then clamped to the breastplate using brass straps and brass wing nuts.

Once the diving suit is secured to the breastplate, lead shoes and a heavy weight belt are placed on the diver. Next, the helmet is placed over the diver's head and secured to the breastplate with a half turn. A safety-locking pin is put in place to prevent the helmet from accidentally separating from the breastplate during the dive.

An air control valve connected to the air supply hose is attached to the breastplate so the diver can control his airflow to the suit. The air flowing to the suit through the helmet not only provides life-giving air for the diver, but it allows the diver to inflate the suit with air. The buoyant lift of the air-filled suit can neutralize the heavily weighted diver and allow him to move freely about on the bottom.

With lots of practice, divers become more skillful at controlling their buoyancy, and they can walk across a soft mud bottom without sinking into it, or they can actually float, suspended in midwater while performing work tasks. Once the helmet is locked in place, only a small round portal (window) called the faceplate, is still open to the outside air. The faceplate is closed and secured before the diver enters the water.

The diver's umbilical, as it is called in diving terminology, consists of a "life-line" and air hose. The air hose delivers air for the diver to breathe. The "life-line" is a rubber coated stainless steel cable containing a set of radio communication wires. The "life-line" not only provides a safety tether for the diver, it also allows voice communication between the diver and the topside crew.

The diver's "life-line" is securely tied to one of the two brass rings on the front of the diver's breastplate with a short length of line called a lanyard. The diver's air hose is tied to the other ring. Both lifeline and air hose are secured in a manner so that any strain taken will be on the lifeline, and not on the air hose. From the breastplate rings, the lifeline and air hose are secured together to make up the diver's umbilical, as it is called in diving terminology.

When we were cleaning and polishing the helmet and breastplate, we removed the lanyards from the brass rings so the rings could be cleaned and polished. At one of our cleaning /maintenance sessions during the first week, John Hardaway, was polishing the breastplate. The holes in the breastplate lanyard rings are almost exactly finger size, and for some reason, known only to the people who do it, John stuck his finger through one of the rings. Almost immediately, his finger swelled slightly, and he was unable to pull his finger out of the ring.

The rest of us in white team were busy with the diving, dress shoes, weight belt, and air hose maintenance. Suddenly, John was among us carrying the breastplate, which was now securely attached with his forefinger through the lanyard ring. He said, " I known this sounds stupid, but I stuck my finger through the lanyard ring and can't get it out." He had a pathetic look on his face as he stood there, cradling the breastplate in his arms!!

When we all stopped laughing, Glen agreed with John that it was a dumb move. I added that it ranked right up there with putting your tongue on frozen metal. Dick said he would get a lot of attention, walking around school for the rest of the day with a Mark Five breastplate attached to his finger. After we had our fun with John, we got some soap and lubricated the lanyard ring so he could pull his finger out. When he was finally free of the breastplate, Dick promptly gave him the nickname of "Lanny the Lanyard." Only the white team would ever know why John was called "Lanny" by his teammates for the rest of the training.

After two weeks of diving equipment orientation, general diving instructions and crew training, we were ready for our first Mark Five dives. Our team leader, Glenn Lewis, went first, then Dick Spear, and then it was my turn to don the big gear. As the helmet was secured in place, the realization hit me that I would be locked inside the copper and brass helmet for over an hour. Before the faceplate was closed and locked, Mr. Mogus leaned down and looked in. "Are you ready?" he asked. "Yes sir," I answered. At that moment, I realized that once the faceplate was closed and secured I would be at the mercy of topside crew.

A diver in heavy gear is totally dependant on the tender to maintain the life supoort systems. If the air supply to a diver is cut off, it is highly unlikely that he could perform the complicated maneuver of cutting himself out of the canvas dress with the few minutes of breathable air left in the helmet. Even if he were able to pull it off, there is still the matter of ascending safely to the surface. It is crucial that the tender understand the dangers of diving work. That is why qualified tenders must also be qualified divers.

The tender closed and secured the faceplate port. I adjusted the control valve and started a flow of cool air into the helmet and suit. I felt my tender place one leg between my knees and take a firm grip on the lifeline and air hose to steady me as I stood up with all that weight. Once I was on my feet, the tender held a short firm grip on the lifeline and air hose, but stood back so I wouldn't step on his feet with the heavy lead shoes. I was then led to the diving ladder at the white team station and turned around with my back facing the water.

My hands were guided to the ladder's railings, which rose about four feet above the diving barge deck. In a few moments I was on the ladder up to my breastplate in water. I paused to make final air adjustments, purge my diving dress of air, and close my spit cock. The spit cock was a small valve on the lower side of the diving helmet. Water could be taken into the helmet through this small valve to wash off the faceplate if it fogged up, or moisten the diver's mouth. It was a mark of a diver's skill to remember to close the spit cock when you entered the water and open it again when you came out.

When my helmet submerged beneath the surface, the initial sensation of diving in the Mark Five deep-sea gear was that of pressure molding the rubberized canvas dress tightly around my body. If you didn't keep a sufficient amount of air flowing into the suit, you got a practical demonstration of the potentially deadly suit squeeze we learned about in diving physics. If you allowed too much air into the suit, it would balloon, and you would have too much buoyancy to allow you to sink. A happy medium between squeeze and buoyancy control is something that a deep sea diver learns in a hurry out of necessity.

After I had reached the bottom rung of the diving ladder and completed my voice communications check, I moved off the ladder and grasped the descending line that led from the barge to the bottom of the estuary. Once I had transferred from the ladder to the descending line, I adjusted my airflow and gave my tender two pulls on the lifeline and air hose. This meant for him to start giving slack so I could descend to the bottom. Even though we could talk to our tender on the radio, we were instructed to use line pull signals between the diver and the tender as a means of primary communication in case of radio failure. After I had given my two pulls, I immediately received two pulls back from my tender and felt the umbilical slack off as I dumped air from the suit and started my descent to the bottom.

On the way down, I needed to clear my ears as the water and air pressure increased. A swallowing, or a chewing motion would accomplish this, but my personal method was to place my upper lip on a small ledge where the helmet joined the breastplate and close off my nostrils. By pushing my upper lip against my nostrils and blowing gently through my nose, I could equalize the pressure.

As I descended the 25 feet to the bottom, I adjusted the air pressure with the control valve and manipulated the "chin button" exhaust valve by pulling it with my mouth and pushing it with my chin. This controlled the amount of air retained, or exhausted, from the suit. My lead shoes finally clanked onto the metal tire rim serving as a descending line weight. I gave one pull, which signaled my tender to stop lowering line and that I was on the bottom.

I ventilated the helmet with a fresh flow of air by opening the control valve and pushing the chin button. This washes out excess carbon dioxide produced by the diver's breathing as he descends. Too much carbon dioxide can incapacitate a diver. After securing the vent, I gave one pull to tell the tender that I was OK.

Next, I heard the voice of Chief Mogus, our instructor. He verified that I was OK, and he asked me to step off the descending line weight and stand away from the line in the mud bottom. I inflated the suit to make it buoyant. Then I stepped back with both feet, dumping some air for weight and stability. Surprise! I immediately sunk in the soft mud up to my waist. My left hand, which was holding the air control-valve was almost resting on top of the mud.

The voice of Chief Mogus echoed inside the helmet. "White diver, are you on the bottom now?" For a moment, I wasn't sure what to tell him, so I said. "White diver is more in the bottom than on it sir!" There was a long moment of silence, and then Chief Mogus came back with a kind of impatient disgust in his voice, "White diver make yourself light, and have your tender pull you out of the mud." I complied, and after some buoyancy adjustments, I was able to keep the mud level at my knees.

The orientation dive wore on and after several training maneuvers, my hour was up and it was time to come to the surface. I inflated my suit with air and came slowly up the descending line. When I neared the surface, I transferred from the line to the diving ladder, and began climbing up the ladder to the barge. When my helmet broke the surface I purged the air from my diving dress, remembering to open my spit cock.

With each step up the ladder the Mark Five gear got heavier and heavier. Both the fatigue of the initial diving exercise, and some water that had leaked into the suit, added extra weight to the climb. With some effort, I reached the top rung and stepped onto the diving deck. The diving gear seemed to be at least twice as heavy as before the dive, and I struggled to make the last six steps to the diver's bench with the aid of my tender. After I turned around, I received the customary two slaps on the helmet to sit down on the bench so that the tenders could take off the helmet. Now I fully understood why tenders must work quickly to help the diver off with heavy diving gear.

One by one, my classmates struggled through their first dive in

Mark Five gear. If any of us had illusions of how glamorous it would be to be a deep sea diver, it was obvious that the glamorous part would come much later. The next two weeks would test each of us to see if we had what it takes to become competent with heavy gear.

CHAPTER 17

Shark Attack

In the first four weeks we practiced many skill-developing exercises. The bottom times got longer, but we were starting to season into the gear, and our control of buoyancy was growing better with each training dive. After a few weeks, we could all move around on the soft mud like it was a hard surface. Once our diving skills were acceptable, we began working with tools and performing various underwater class projects. By this time we could suspend ourselves in mid-water with our buoyancy control and swim laterally through the water column without the aid of our tenders. Our underwater projects varied from working with hand tools to a variety of pneumatically operated power tools. We learned to work with underwater concrete and to cut and weld underwater.

The training progressed, and so did our confidence and skill to perform underwater work in deep-sea diving gear. We learned the physics and physiology of diving, how to run the decompression chamber and to treat divers in the chamber if they manifested symptoms of decompression sickness, commonly known as "the bends." We learned basic seamanship and diving salvage. We learned about all the underwater work that divers are required to perform.

During the four months at Deep Sea School there were many memorable experiences, but one in particular stands out vividly in my mind. It was around the fourth or fifth week of training and we had pretty much mastered our buoyancy control and could now effectively move about on the soft mud bottom. We were conducting bottom sweep searches. This is where the diver pulls about 125 feet of lifeline and air hose straight out away from his tender until he is stopped with a line pull signal. The diver is then put on searching signals—a special set of signals to guide him left or right in an arc across the bottom while he searches for some lost object.

The tender watches the diver's bubbles as the arc covers the probable search area. The diver is given a signal to stop and allowed to ventilate and rest for a couple of minutes. Pulling over 100 feet of lifeline and air hose on the bottom sweep search is strenuous work when the diver is walking on a soft mud bottom. Once the diver has ventilated and rested, the tender takes up about 3 feet of umbilical and gives the diver a signal to travel an arc in the opposite direction.

The arcs move in toward the tender with each sweep and somewhat overlap. Using this method the diver can cover nearly every square foot of bottom in the search area. Once the diver stomps his way across the bottom, he stirs up a lot of mud and debris. What little visibility was available in the green gray water of the estuary fades to an opaque mix of mud and water.

After the first arc is completed, the rest of the search is done pretty much by Braille. The diver has to put out his hand and feel the bottom ahead of him as he moves across the arc. At times, the density of the thick mud blocks all visibility and leaves only enough light to barely see the inside of the helmet. It's kind of spooky running your light cotton gloved hand out into the mud ahead of you in near total darkness. This was of some concern, because Mr. Mogus told us before the diving searches started that dead bodies are sometimes found in the estuary. He said that we should have our tender notify him if we thought we had found one.

As if the thought of coming helmet to face with a corpse wasn't enough to test your nerves, he also mentioned casually that fairly large sharks sometimes came into the estuary. Although disturbing, I thought the odds of finding a body were pretty low, but the shark thing had me a little spooked.

There were lots of sharks in the ocean and out in the San Francisco Bay. They moved around a lot, and the idea of encountering some in the estuary seemed plausible to me. Every time I reached the end of the sweep, ventilated and took my two minutes rest, I thought about the white cotton gloves I was wearing and how they might attract a large shark.

During my rest at the end of the next sweep, I was plagued by the "shark thought" again. I have always disciplined myself to overcome any fears by directly confronting them. Unknown to me, an unintentional, but diabolical coincidence was developing.

Our radio man topside had noticed that white diver (me) and blue diver (Tex) had come to the end of our arcs just a few yards from each other. Of course, neither one could see the other because of all the silt stirred up from our searches. Topside asked blue diver if he could see me and told him that I was just a few yards to his left as he faced the tended air hose. The silt was beginning to settle down and a slight current cleared the water somewhat. Once it cleared up to its maximum potential, you could still only see about half the distance of the length of your arm. If I fully extended my arm, my white cotton glove would disappear in the grey-green gloom.

I had just finished my ventilation and was resting, waiting for my tender to give me the signal for the next sweep. As I stood there on the bottom, peering out the upper port of the helmet into the water, I began to have shark thoughts again. After a few moments of shark anxiety, I became very annoyed with myself for letting my imagination get the better of me. On the spot, I resolved to master this fear right there and then, so I thrust out my right arm and white-gloved hand, and waved it around vigorously while mentally challenging any marauding sharks in the vicinity to take their best shot.

It was precisely at this time that blue diver, who was standing on the mud ridge slightly above my location, saw my white gloved hand thrust up into view through his front helmet port. He immediately reached out and grasped my hand with both of his. At that moment I thought my challenge had been answered, and, for a few seconds, everything in my body that could pucker did so—violently! In a flash, blue diver had pulled himself down the mud bank to me, and our helmets clanked together.

After my heart had receded from my throat and I realized what was really happening, we turned our airflows down very low, touched our helmets and began talking to each other through the diving helmets without the aid of electronic communication. The first thing I said to blue diver is not fit to repeat! Suffice to say that everyone in Jack London Square in earshot of the diver's radio knew that I had been surprised.

As I was being dressed out of my gear after the dive, Mr. Mogus came up to me with a huge grin on his face and asked me if I had survived the shark attack? I looked up at him sheepishly, and said, "Nothing hurt, but my pride sir." I told him what had happened and he took one of his big hands, ruffled my hair, and said, " It's OK, son, that would have scared the crap out of me too." I felt a little better, but I was still embarrassed!

Diving school was over and our final projects were done and graded. Graduation was only a few days away and we were mainly cleaning up our gear and making plans to look for diving work. Mr. Mogus gathered us all together in the classroom and told us that we were one of the best classes he had ever had at the school. Maybe he told that to all the graduating classes, but I doubt it because he was a man of integrity. We all liked and respected Chief Mogus. He was a tough taskmaster and demanded discipline and maximum effort from all of us, but we knew that he wanted us to be safe and proficient as commercial divers.

Deep sea diving school was a special experience that can only be fully understood by another deep sea diver. As I walked up to the boarding house from school for the last time, I turned and looked out on Jack London Square and the training barge next to the school dock. Soon another class would be dressing into their diving gear, coiling lifeline and air hose and developing the discipline it takes to become a graduate of deep sea diving school. I would kind of miss it, but I was glad it was over.

My mental trip to deep-sea diving school was interrupted by the sound of the boat lock gates opening and suddenly I was back at Ice Harbor Dam. I raised my head to see that several other small boats had come alongside to enter the locks. In a few minutes we would all take a water elevator ride down to the river level below the dam.

When the gates were fully open the Lockmaster ushered in the boats, one at a time. Ordinarily, no one would be allowed to swim in the lock while the water was being lowered, but since I had to remain in the water as much as possible, the officials at the dam made an exception for me, as long as I would agree to remain next to our boat.

It was an interesting experience going through the locks. I just floated in the water, next to the *No-Name*, and talked with a lot of the boaters who were surprised to find me in the locks with them. After being lowered about 100 feet to the river below the dam, the lock gates opened. When all the boats had exited the lock, I was allowed to swim out into the main river channel toward my Tri Cities rendezvous. As I passed through the gates the Lockmaster wished me good luck and I flashed him a high sign.

It was about 8 miles from the locks to the bridge where I was to meet a big cabin cruiser from Metz Marina. By the time I made the final swim to the bridge, I had been awake for about 28 hours, 18 of them spent swimming in the river. I swam to the bridge and touched the concrete support pier. Within minutes the big cabin cruiser arrived and took me aboard. I was very tired and I kind of collapsed from exhaustion. I'm afraid I didn't provide a very good interview for the media that was at Metz Marina to meet me. I kept spacing out and dozing off between questions, so I excused myself and promised to give them better stories after I had some sleep.

After a few hours of rest, and some much-needed food, I was taken to participate in several Water Follies activities and was again interviewed by local radio and television stations. I enjoyed the festivities and the media attention, but I was very tired and my thoughts were never far from the miles and miles of river still left to swim.

CHAPTER 18

Bill Harris Divers

The next stretch of river was from the Tri-Cities to Walulla Junction, a distance of about 13 miles. We stopped there because of high winds on the reservoir and returned to the Tri-Cities. It was a short day, but I didn't mind because it gave me an opportunity to recuperate from the damage done in the Snake. The next day the weather was overcast, and no better than the day before. I planned to swim the entire length of the McNary Reservoir, called Lake Wallula. It was about a 25 mile swim in almost still water, against strong upriver winds.

The winds were strong enough to make white-capped waves on the reservoir. The day turned into a constant, monotonous, and fatiguing grind. I still felt some pain from the damage done to my body in the upriver rapids, but after several hours of swimming, the pain was overshadowed by fatigue. Most of the day my head was totally submerged with just the end of the snorkel sticking slightly above the surface.

I swam for hours with a modified sidestroke. An Army Corps of Engineers boat traveled along next to us for a couple of hours and logged my average speed at 4.5 knots. I was surprised that I was able to keep up that speed for over two hours. An average walking speed is about three miles an hour, and it's a lot easier to walk than swim against wind and waves.

I used the side of the *No-Name* for guidance, so I wouldn't have to keep lifting my head to look downriver for my direction. There were times when I would enter a semi-hypnotic state, induced by visual fixation on the white hull of the boat and the steady, rhythmic, porpoise-like motion of my body surfing through the water. I wasn't fully conscious of anything except the hull of the boat, water flowing past my mask, my regular breathing, echoing in the snorkel tube, and the mesmerizing pace of the swimming stroke. At times some disturbance, or a call from the boat crew, would break the trance-like state and I would be amazed to find that two or three hours had elapsed since I last looked up!

We arrived at our destination about two miles from McNary Dam and pulled into a small dock where we were met by our host and taken to Umatilla, Oregon. We were treated to a fine dinner at a local restaurant and then taken to a hotel for the night. The meal was great and the hotel accommodations were comfortable but I didn't sleep very well that night and I had a vivid dream about starting work as a deep-sea diver.

When I left deep-sea diving school there was an opportunity to go to the Gulf States and try to get work with one of the diving companies that were specializing in the booming offshore oil business. At that time it would have been a ground-floor opportunity, but I chose to go to Spokane where Susan was now living with her family. They had recently moved to Spokane from Clarkston, Washington. My plan was eventually to move to the Seattle area and look for diving work there. Once I returned to Spokane, I became focused mainly on surviving as I had no money and no job. Susan's folks, Doc and Jean Craig, were wonderful people and they allowed me to stay with them for a couple of weeks until I found temporary work.

I found a job as a copywriter for a direct sales company that sold a famous brand of cookware door to door. My job was to assist the editor of the company magazine and write motivational articles about the success of their salespeople. It was an interesting job and paid adequately, but my mind and heart were set on becoming a professional diver.

After three months as a copywriter, I had almost resigned myself to the fact that I would have to work long enough to save some money and move to Seattle before I would find any type of diving work. As luck would have it, my copywriter job required me to check the want ads of the Spokane paper because the company was always advertising for salespeople.

It was an early July morning and I was checking the wording and accuracy of the company help wanted ad when I almost fell out of my chair. One ad in another column read, "Wanted Commercial Deep Sea Diver, heavy diving gear qualified, chamber qualified, U.S. Navy or commercial diving school certificate required. Contact Bill Harris Divers, Phone #, Spokane, Washington." The ad blew me away. I never thought in my wildest dreams that someone in Spokane would be advertising for a deep sea diver! At my next break, I called the number.

A woman with a pleasant voice answered and identified herself as Bill Harris' wife, Elaine. She was surprised that they would get a response so soon. She had just placed the ad the day before. She asked me a few questions about my training and background, and then she told me that Bill and the crew were in Wyoming working on the Buffalo Bill Cody hydroelectric dam. She would relay my information to him when he checked in with her on his routine evening call. She took my home number and said Bill would want to talk to me. The rest of that day was agony for me as I could think of nothing else but the possibility that I might soon have my first job as commercial diver.

About 7:00 p.m. that night the phone rang. A voice on the other end said. "Hello, this is Bill Harris—is this Spence?" "Yes sir," I replied.

Bill asked a few questions about my background and schooling. He asked me what kind of grades I got in Diving Physiology, Treatment Tables and Chamber Operation. Fortunately, those were the areas where I scored 100%. He then explained that they were working in very deep water on the upstream face of the Buffalo Bill Cody Dam in the reservoir. He said all the divers were making very deep dives requiring a lot of decompression.

Decompression requires the diver to make stops at various depths upon returning to the surface. It allows the nitrogen gas compressed into the diver's tissues and blood during the dive to escape gradually without causing decompression sickness, or by its common name, "The Bends." He also said that the decompression was complicated by the dam's elevation, nearly a mile high.

Divers making deep dives in high altitude lakes have to compensate for the fact that they are surfacing to a reduced atmospheric pressure. The decompression required is different because the altitude causes the dive to equate to a deeper depth. He said they were using some experimental surface decompression tables bootlegged from the Navy and he wanted to know whether I could handle running the chamber for special decompression and treatments if necessary. I said that I was light on experience, but heavy on desire, and would do whatever it took to get up to speed for the operation.

There was a long moment of silence and then Bill said, "My wife, Elaine will have some airline tickets for you day after tomorrow. I need you here by Friday. Can you make it?" "See you Friday, sir," I replied. After I hung up with Bill, my mind did several back-flips in celebration, and I immediately called Susan to tell her the great news.

First thing the next morning I informed my present employer about the opportunity and apologized for having to leave on short notice, as it was not my normal way of doing things. The next day I drove to Bill Harris' house and picked up my tickets from Elaine. She also gave me some packages and a box of parts to take to Bill at the job.

The small commuter plane arrived at the Cody, Wyoming airport at about 4:00 p.m. on Friday afternoon. Bill Harris, and his son, Noel, were there to meet me. Bill was a medium built man about 5'10" with black hair and weathered, but pleasant face. He greeted me with a big smile and a warm friendly demeanor. He shook my hand and introduced me to his son.

Noel was a tall, large-boned, blonde lad of 19, with the same friendly warmth of his dad. We picked up my suitcase and Bill's packages and then drove into Cody to the motel where the crew was staying. While we drove, Bill explained why he needed to hire another diver so urgently. It seems that they were within three weeks of completing the diving job and one of his divers had been getting repeated attacks of the bends.

The dives they were making were now over 200 feet and the daily decompression had taken its toll on one of his older divers. He had to undergo treatment in the decompression chamber for several cases of the bends in a period of three weeks. In order to treat a diver for severe decompression sickness, treatment time required in the chamber is over 19 hours. Even if the treatment is successful, it is debilitating to the diver and very stressful on the tender if one is required to accompany a disabled diver in the chamber. Needless to say, Bill was anxious to avoid having to treat the divers.

That first evening we had a good dinner at the local restaurant and I had a chance to associate with the other divers on the team. One diver was an ex-Navy first class diver who had worked with Bill for several years and had a lot of hydroelectric dam diving experience. They had done work on several big dams across the Northwest, including the Grand Coulee Dam on the Columbia River. Over dinner he and Bill recounted some great diving stories about work done on the various dams.

Some of the stories were pretty intense and exciting in a scary way, but I knew by the manner in which they were told that they were not intended to intimidate me. They were just work-a-day occurrences that spice up the life of a commercial deep sea diver. We wound down the day with a couple more stories then retired to our rooms at the motel.

It was a weekend and several key support personnel at the dam were gone, so we would just be doing some maintenance. I would have a couple of days to get familiar with the operation and equipment. The next day we drove up to the job site at Buffalo Bill Cody Dam. The dam is located in a steep walled canyon and dams up the water of the South fork of the Shoshone River. This huge concrete dam wedged into the steep canyon walls is an impressive sight.

The diving operations barge was about 50 feet wide and 60 feet long, and contained our decompression chamber, which measured 17 feet long and 7 feet in diameter. It was an old caisson chamber formerly used for "sandhogs," a name given to men who work digging huge tunnels under rivers or other bodies of water. Those men have to work under increased air pressure to keep the water from flooding the tunnel. Because they work full shifts under increased atmospheric pressures, they must decompress slowly, just like divers who have performed a deep dive, or have been under increased water pressure for long periods of time.

The barge also housed our air compressors, air storage tanks, and our diving support equipment. A small boat with an open back deck and a cabin forward was moored alongside the big barge. It served as a platform for dressing in and launching the divers. We did some maintenance work and organized the diving platform so we could begin diving operations on Monday morning.

In the afternoon I had a break and I sat on the staging boat staring down onto the surface of the water. It was hard for me to imagine that at the start of the job, the reservoir depth was about 140 feet and now at the end of the project, the divers were working in over 200 feet of water!

The water level had risen steadily during the job requiring new maximum working times and compensating decompression schedules.

The more sophisticated diving equipment and technology used by today's commercial diving companies would have eliminated a lot of the problems that we encountered using compressed air for deep diving, but in 1959 few civilian diving companies had the equipment, or the technology, to perform deep dives using helium and oxygen instead of compressed air. At that time the technology was still under development by the U.S. Navy.

While I stared into the dark water, my mind created a scenario of what would be like to make a 200-foot dive to the bottom of this muddy, debris filled reservoir. Once in the water the diver would follow a line to the work area below. Ten feet below the surface the diver would lose all light and be immersed in total darkness. At 40 feet, the diver would pass through an abrupt temperature change called the thermo cline, and the water would turn very cold. Passing 50 feet, the pressure would increase and the air would warm and thicken noticeably. The diver would then gradually increase the airflow to prevent the suit from squeezing his lower extremities, and he would adjust his buoyancy to control his descent speed.

At 100 feet the air would grow warmer and thicker, and in spite of the precautionary filtering of the air, any impurities would be detected more by taste than by smell. At 175 feet, the diver would be able to detect the metallic taste of the nitrogen in the air. The air would now warm considerably and cause a relaxing and euphoric effect. Any anxiety or apprehension that diver may have had prior to the dive would fade to a warm fuzzy feeling, similar to having a couple of potent alcoholic drinks on an empty stomach. This is why this effect on a diver called "nitrogen narcosis" is nicknamed "Martini's Law."

Passing 200 feet, the combined effects of narcosis, carbon dioxide build up from the diver's breathing during the long descent, and the total darkness of the environment, would create a disorienting effect.

Once on the bottom, the diver would stop and ventilate his helmet with a flow of air. The cooler air flowing around his face would lower the carbon dioxide and somewhat clear his head, reducing the severe effects of nitrogen narcosis. Now the diver would try to orient himself to the work area and attempt to accomplish the underwater tasks he was assigned.

To stay focused on the work at hand and resist the effects of deep diving in over 200 feet of water on compressed air would require effort and discipline from the diver, and not all divers have the same level of tolerance to function effectively. There are some divers who can produce useful work at deep depths, while others are seriously incapacitated. Diving companies know which of their divers are best suited for deep air work.

In my mind's eye, I could see the diver moving about on the bottom and going about his work as best he could. My mind then surfaced from the mental dive, and I went back to my afternoon work of preparing the diving station.

Only a few weeks of deep diving work was left on the project when I joined the crew. In those weeks I tended the divers, and ran the decompression chamber. Tending surface supplied divers using heavy gear in over 200 feet of water was hard work! The lifeline and air hose umbilical weighs over a half pound per foot. Lowering the diver that far down is hard. Pulling the diver up again is even harder!

While the diver descends, the supervisor keeps in constant communication with him on the radio. The deep depth effects the diver's voice is and it becomes very nasal. The diver must speak slowly and distinctly to be understood by the topside crew. Line pull signals between the tender and the diver become ineffective because of the long length and weight of the umbilical.

The work we were performing at the time was installing "Trash Racks." These are large, metal cage-like structures that prevent logs and debris from entering the intake wells. This is where the water is taken into tubes that lead to the huge water-driven electric turbine generators.

The deepwater diving work was taking its toll on our older

divers and I had to run several decompression sickness treatment schedules for one diver who had several attacks of the bends. Bill had to release him from the job before it was completed for his own safety and that left us short one diver.

I thought maybe I would get a chance to dive on the project since we were short a diver, but there was not enough time for me to break out on this job, particularly at such deep depths and with no experience with the structures we were working on. I seem to understand chamber operations and treatment procedures better than anyone else on the job, so I was needed more in the topside crew.

The Cody Dam job ended all too quickly for me. Even though I had made some decent money on the job, I wasn't sure the money would hold out until another diving job came along. Bill said that there was a possible job coming up at the Garrison Dam on the Missouri River in North Dakota. He said that it would be about a week before he knew whether he had the job and about a month before the job would start. He told me not to worry, and not to look for a job, that he had work for me when we got back to Spokane. That was good news and made me feel more secure.

Back in Spokane, Bill, Noel, and I spent the next month renovating diving equipment. We sandblasted and painted the decompression chamber and fitted out the huge trailer with all of our diving equipment. When we were done, Bill had a professional sign painter paint a large Mark Five Helmet and Bill Harris Divers Company sign on the decompression chamber.

With all equipment cleaned and polished, the big chamber and air volume tank painted powder blue, the helmet logo, and a new red Apache truck with company signs on the doors, we looked and felt like a million bucks. After fitting out our equipment, Bill had us paint his house to keep us working. By now, we knew that we had the Garrison Dam job and it was only two weeks before we would be off to North Dakota.

During the last week before leaving for the new diving job, I spent most of my time off with Susan. Our romance got serious enough for me to propose to her and we sealed our engagement before I left for North Dakota. Bill and I would be the only ones going on this job from Spokane, but we would be joined by one other diver at the job site. Walter O'Shell, was a Navy First Class Petty Officer and First Class Diver on leave from the Naval recruiting office in Billings, Montana. He had been accepted and was waiting for a class at officer candidate school. He and I would be the divers on this job.

On the long drive from Spokane to Garrison, North Dakota, I had the opportunity to get to know Bill Harris, the man. Things that stand out in my mind about Bill are his sense of fairness and his fierce concern for the safety and welfare of his divers and crew. Bill's philosophy was that divers do hard, dangerous work, and sometimes they endure extremely unpleasant and painful conditions. They were, therefore, entitled to the best food, lodging, and treatment he could afford.

Bill knew all the best restaurants between Spokane and the Missouri River. He used to keep a small guidebook by Duncan Hines, a connoisseur of fine foods who traveled about the country discovering places that serve great meals. Whenever we entered a restaurant, Bill would immediately ask for the manager. He would tell him that he wanted the best and the largest steaks they had. He said that he wanted them done to perfection and that "price was no object." Most often we would get a superb steak and great tasting accompanying dishes. Bill had a magical way of bringing out the best service from all the places where we stopped.

He was almost fanatic about the food and service rendered to his crew. Bill always paid top dollar for the food, and would tip lavishly if the service was prompt and courteous. He would never fail to complement the manager on the food and service if it was deserved. Only on rare occasions would we get substandard service or poor food.

Bill made no bones about chastising the manager for the bad food or service. He could do it in such a way that if the manager really cared about the quality of the cuisine, he would usually comp the meal. Bill would then complement him on his fairness and vow to return to give them another try. In this situation he would usually leave money to pay for the table service.

Always true to his word, Bill would make it a point to return to that restaurant, call out the manager, and make his famous request for the "biggest and best; cost being no object." He would also remind the manager that he appreciated his integrity the last time we were there.

Bill's approach worked wonders. I have no idea what transpired between the manager and his chefs and staff, but the return meal was always wonderful and done to perfection. When the meal was over, Bill would complement and compensate everyone at the restaurant. Everywhere that Bill went, the managers greeted him by name. Even those with whom Bill had altercations seemed to admire him, and were eager to please him when he returned.

CHAPTER 20

Dam Divers

It took a couple of days to drive to the Garrison Dam. When we arrived our other diver, Walt O'Shell, was waiting for us at the hotel. We had dinner at a local restaurant and Bill briefed us on the job. There was a prime contractor for the overall work and we would be subcontracting for them.

The job involved detecting and sealing some leaks in the draft tube gates. These gates consist of a number of concrete rectangular logs that are about 15 feet long and 4 feet square stacked upon each other to seal off the draft tube. Draft tubes are square concrete tunnel openings on the downstream side of the dam. The turbulent discharge of water from the draft tube tunnels into the river just below the dam is called the tailrace.

Water taken from deep in the reservoir flows through tunnels that pass through the dam; they're called penstocks. The water passes through the dam and turns the turbine generators like a high-speed waterwheel. The water then flows out of the dam through the draft tubes into the river below the dam.

The dam is designed so that the engineers can seal off the penstock.

They seal off draft tube openings with permanently installed gates, or temporary barriers called stop logs. They can prevent water from entering the penstocks by closing the upstream gates in the reservoir. The entire tunnel from the reservoir through the dam to the draft tube can then be dewatered with powerful scavenger pumps. This allows the engineers to go down into the draft tubes and inspect them when they are dry.

Bill explained that there was so much leakage from the gates that the scavenger pumps could not overcome the rate at which water was entering the tunnels. The diver's job was to find the leak points and seal them if possible so that the tubes could be dewatered.

Another task would require a dive on the upstream side of the dam to about 160 feet to inspect the trash racks. Trash racks are large cage-like structures that cover the entrance to the penstocks and keep sunken logs and debris from passing through the tunnels and damaging the turbines. The diver would have to clear away any debris blocking the flow of water through the trash track grates and inspect for damage done due to vibration.

The next morning we arrived on the job and set up the diving stations. It was late October and the weather was overcast and cold. After setting up and testing the diving gear, Bill said we would make an inspection dive. Walt would make the first dive, and I would tend. Walt and I would then alternate dives. After Walt inspected and installed the stop logs for one draft tube it was decided that we should do one more unit before quitting for the day.

Now it was my turn! Dressing into the heavy gear again felt familiar and strange at the same time. It had been almost six months since my last dive in heavy gear and as the helmet was secured in place I felt a little apprehension knowing that this was my first real commercial dive and I was about to be tested on the job. I stood up from the diving bench and stepped onto the lowering platform, which we called the diver's stage.

I felt vulnerable standing there on a small metal platform hanging

On the diving stage waiting to be lowered

50 feet above the surface of the water in the big heavy gear. Any time a diver rides a stage from considerable height to the water, there's always a potential danger of being dropped or falling. In heavy gear that could have fatal consequences.

The ride down to the water was smooth and uneventful, and soon I was up to my breastplate in the dark waters of the Missouri River. The stage stopped as the water reached the faceplate on the helmet. After adjusting my airflow and buoyancy I transferred to the descending line leading down to the worksite. I closed my spitcock, gave my tender two pulls, and started my descent. The dim light penetrated the murky water to about 6 feet where it faded to total darkness. At this point I had to shift to a different level of orientation. It was necessary to abandon the need to see with my eyes and create a mental picture of my surroundings from previously studied plans and photographs.

When I reached the top of the draft tube gate at a depth of 50 feet, I ventilated the helmet. The combined effects of the heavy suit

Riding the stage 50 feet down to the water

and helmet insulating and protecting me from the water, and the thick inky blackness, gave me a feeling of being isolated. I felt sort of safely tucked away in a small metal room with only my gloved hands projecting into the semi-dangerous environment.

My first task was to work my way across the top of the gate and release a 30-pound metal shackle from the lifting eye in the stop-log. To stay oriented in the total darkness I crawled along the top of the four-foot concrete log, guiding myself along its length by feeling the outside edge of the log with my gloved hands.

We were using the suits with the attached gloves because the water was quite cold this time of year. We preferred to use suits without gloves because we could have more dexterity with our hands, but this cold water would have quickly numbed the hands, making it dangerous to handle heavy rigging or sharp metal objects. If a diver loses feeling in his hands he could easily lose fingers, or a hand, if he is careless.

During the 15-foot crawl to the other end of the stop log, my body was almost in a horizontal position. I reached the lifting eye on the far side and my helmet came into contact with the big steel shackle and the lifting cable running up to the crane on the surface. When I located the shackle, I began to position it so I could unscrew the shackle pin and release it from the lifting eye. The shackle was heavy, and I had to twist the shackle around and work against its weight and the weight of three or four feet of heavy cable to get it into a position where I could unscrew the pin.

Everything a diver does such as pushing or pulling is met with an opposing force pushing back on the diver due to his weightless condition of neutral buoyancy. Because the diver needs weight to achieve a working leverage, he exhausts air from the suit to make him heavy. At this time I had exhausted quite a bit of air from the suit, and it was squeezing me snugly from the feet up to the breastplate.

My head was raised up against the back of the inside of the helmet as I struggled to get the shackle and cable adjusted to where I could remove the pin. During this maneuver my body was almost horizontal and the top of my helmet was tilted slightly downward. I finally got the shackle positioned and the pin removed and was able to relax from the effort. As I brought my head forward from the back of the helmet, my face was completely submerged in water. A two-word expletive came immediately to my mind, and for a brief moment I had visions of my helmet flooding! Having your face covered with cold water in a pitch black diving helmet can cause severe anxiety, if not downright panic. My reaction was that of shock and total surprise. I immediately struggled to my feet pulling myself up by the lifting cable attached to the shackle.

The considerable amount of water that had leaked into the helmet then went down into the suit bib, but most of it overflowed into the suit, soaking the front of my chest and stomach with cold water. I must have yelled out, or made some bizarre noise when I thought I was drowning, because no sooner had I jumped to my feet than Bill's voice came over the radio, "Spence! Are you ok?" Before responding to Bill's query, I suddenly realized where all water came from.

When I descended from the surface down the lifting cable to the stop log gate, I must have tripped open my spit cock. While I was lying prone, face down with my head pressed against the back of the helmet and had my air reduced to make me heavier, water had slowly poured in through the open spit cock, putting about 5 inches of water in the bottom half of the helmet! Bill's voice rung out again, "Spence! Are you ok?" "Nothing serious," I replied. "I just got a big shot of cold water!" Since divers periodically get leaks in the diving dress, a cold shot of water is not of much concern to anyone except the cold wet diver.

The rest of my first commercial dive went great. After about three hours of work on the bottom, the stop logs were set, and the inspection was completed. I signaled my tender to take up the slack, and I was brought back from the thick, black confinement of the river bottom to the top side world of light and fresh air. I was pretty cold, but happy and proud that I was now a working deep sea diver.

The ringing of the phone next to my bed interrupted my dreams about the Garrison Dam dives. It was the 5:30 a.m. wake up call from the hotel switchboard. When the phone was silent I tried to get fully awake, but I felt very fatigued, like I'd been diving all night.

At breakfast, I thought about Bill Harris and his wife Elaine. I wondered if they were following the swim and if they thought I had lost my mind. With breakfast over, I put on my wet suit and we were taken to our boat moored just above the dam. Because of the fatigue and the restless night, I wasn't looking forward to swimming another 30 or 40 miles.

CHAPTER 21

The Columbia

The next morning a good-sized crowd came to see us as we passed through the locks of the McNary Dam and started our trip down the mighty Columbia. During the next three days, I swam from McNary Dam to Boardman Oregon, then from Boardman to Arlington and from Arlington to the John Day River. The total distance was about 70 miles. During those three days nothing dangerous or spectacular happened, and that was ok by me! It was just hours of hard swimming, and I noticed that I was losing a lot of weight. Swimming 557 miles down the Clearwater, Snake, and Columbia Rivers will definitely trim your body, but it's a killer weight loss program and I don't recommend it.

On the first day the river was rolling along nicely and I was able to use a resting stroke most of the time. When the river was docile like that the swim became hours and hours of boredom, and my mind wandered a lot. Because of the diving dream I had a few nights before, my thoughts seemed to be focused on those first few jobs as a diver on the dams. The drone of the jet boat engine and the easy rolling motion took me back to the Garrison Dam.

We finished our first week of diving and the weather got colder and colder. The Corps of Engineers elected not to work over the weekend so we had a couple of days off. The weather continued to deteriorate over the weekend and the sky became dark and overcast. If it began to freeze, it would make very unpleasant conditions for the diving crew.

On Sunday night we all went to bed early and set our clocks for an early morning diving day. My room was on the ground floor and it had a small window that looked out into a garden courtyard. Before I went to bed I drew the shade and left it a couple of inches up so I would have some light to see by in the early morning.

The alarm clock went off way too early Monday morning and I reluctantly rolled out of bed. The room was dark except for a little light streaming in through the narrow opening below the drawn shade. I stopped in front of the window and raised the shade to let in the morning light. Imagine my surprise when I found myself staring into a blanket of pristine snow, which was only about one foot below the base of the window. I was dumbfounded! I dressed quickly, and wondered how this would affect the diving job. When I joined Bill and Walt for breakfast, Bill cursed the luck of the weather, but he said if the Corps of Engineers wanted to continue the work today, then we would dive! Bill must have had a sixth sense about the weather because he insisted that we bring heavy clothing and foul weather gear with us. Because Bill was from North Dakota, he would know about the weather there, and I'm glad he did!

The Corps of Engineers put us on standby until they took care of some snow removal work, but by 1:30 p.m. in the afternoon they were ready to have us start diving. It was Walt's turn to dive; his job was to try to seal leaks in the draft tube gates so the draft tube tunnels could be pumped dry. As I dressed Walt for the dive, the temperature dropped steadily. The weather forecast said there was a powerful cold front moving into the area.

As the afternoon diving progressed, the lifeline and air hose started freezing and sticking together as I laid the coils down on the snow covered concrete floor of the staging area. Diving was cold, and somewhat miserable, but tending was brutal! As I handled the wet umbilical, the water soaked my flimsy cotton gloves and began to freeze.

After a couple of hours I told Bill that I had to get my hands warm for fear of frostbite. Bill went to his truck and got me a pair of warm, dry mittens. It was about the third hour of tending in the numbing cold that I began to question the wisdom of my chosen profession. I also noticed that my diver, Walt, was showing signs of hypothermia. He had been underwater for almost three hours. I recommended to Bill that we get him topside and warm him up; Bill agreed and told us to terminate the dive. When we were undressing Walt we could see that he was definitely suffering from hypothermia. Walt never complained about being cold, but it was kind of an unwritten code among divers that you didn't wimp out.

The contractor foreman saw us bring up the diver. He came to the diving station and shouted at Bill about stopping the work. Bill explained that the long exposures in the cold water were creating a potential serious medical problem for the diver and we needed to get him warmed up.

The foreman continued to protest about stopping the work and then made some crack about divers being sissies and primadonna's. That did it. In less than two seconds Bill was standing toe to toe with the foreman declaring that he was not going to jeopardize the safety or health of his divers for anyone!

In a voice that was unmistakably scalding mad, he told the foreman that he would gladly dress him into Mark Five gear, put him on the bottom in total darkness for three hours in this freezing water, and then get a second opinion about who was a sissy and a primadonna. The ferocity of Bill's verbal attack on the foreman took him by surprise. He stood looking at Bill for a long moment, then without saying a word, he turned around and walked away.

Obviously, Bill made his point and the challenge went unaccepted. In an evening meeting with the prime contractor and the Corps of Engineers, the Corps' Safety and Medical Officers supported Bill's position and mandated that the working times for the divers be limited to safe exposures for the extreme temperature conditions.

Over the next two weeks of the job Walt and I alternated as diver and tender. The inspections and leaks sealing operations went well and the weather warmed up a bit—thank God!

About two days into the last week of the job Walt was sealing gate leaks in one of the units. The leaks mainly occur at the base of the gates and because of the difference in pressure from the 50 feet of water outside the draft tube gate to about 25 feet of water on the inside of the draft tube gate, a huge and very dangerous suction is created at the leak site.

We were locating the leaks by using a three-foot stick with a number of long rag strips attached to one end. The diver drags this "ribbon wand," as we called it, along the bottom of the gate and when the cloth streamers are sucked into the leaks, the diver feels the pull on the stick. Once the leak is located, the diver seals the leak with a concoction called tarred hemp, which he carries in a bucket. This is a thick mixture of heavy bits of manila line and congealed tar. This stuff is sticky and heavy and the weight of the tar keeps it from floating out of the bucket. Knowing the position of the leak he dumps the sealing material close to the leak site and the suction pulls it in, sealing the leak. With small leaks sometimes the diver will take handfuls of the material and release it near the leak.

During the sealing operations the diver must be extra careful not to get his hand too close to the leak site. The difference in pressure could actually force a diver's fingers and arm into a small crack under the concrete gate mangling his arm and trapping him there. This would pretty much seal the fate of the diver.

Walt was patching leaks when I heard him cry out over the

radio. I immediately queried him on his condition, but he didn't answer. I got only muffled sounds of a struggle punctuated with some grunts and barely audible profanity! Again, I queried the diver. "Walt! Are you ok?" Again, there was only muffled struggling sounds, and then silence! I called to Bill—"We have a diver in trouble here!" Bill stopped tending our air compressor and ran toward the diving station. I was just starting to pull Walt up when I heard his voice call out over the radio, "Hold it. "Hold it! I'm ok now, but my suit is flooding. Bring me up to the stage!" Walt felt extra heavy as I pulled him up from the 50-foot depth. When he reached the surface he climbed onto the stage and we winched him up to the tending station some 50 feet above the water. When we got him on deck I could see that his bare right arm was hanging out of a jagged short sleeve of the torn diving dress. The sleeve and heavy glove were gone from just below the elbow.

Once we got the helmet off, a concerned, but unusually calm Walt explained what happened. He was placing some sealing material on a fairly large leak when a blast of current from the nearby operating unit pushed him against the gate. Instinctively, he put out his right hand to regain balance and control, but his hand was too close to the leak. The next thing he knew his glove was being sucked into the crack. He was barely able to get his hand out of the glove and withdrawn up the arm of the dress before his fingers were trapped and sucked in with the glove. He tried to pull the glove free, but the suction was too strong. It was then he realized that the glove and the arm of the dress were still being slowly pulled into the crack. At that point he got a little exited and really started pulling hard.

Fortunately, the seam where the glove attached to the dress tore loose and ripped the glove off the sleeve. Now he was free, but the ice-cold water was pouring into the suit. He said that he had been so occupied with his survival during the ordeal that he didn't realized I had been trying to contact him on the radio.

As Walt related this close call, a cold realization hit me. What would have happened if Walt's hand had been sucked into the crack along with the glove? If pressure wasn't equalized on both sides of the gate soon enough by the engineers at the dam, (which was highly unlikely), Walt might have had to lose fingers or a hand to get free. Now, I was starting to gain insight to the profound dangers in commercial diving. After a couple more days of diving in the freezing weather we completed the diving job and went home to Spokane.

Memories of diving on the dams was interrupted when a small cabin cruiser came alongside the *No-Name* and started talking to my crew. There were about six people in the boat and looking out from the cabin window was a young woman with a small child in her arms. She was holding the baby's arm, waving to me with its' small hand. I pulled up from my swimming stroke and waved back. The sight of this mother with her child made me think about Susan and my small son.

Swimmer At Half-Way Mark, Finds Columbia 'Ferocious'

ARLINGTON, Ore. — Marathon swimmer **Spencer** Campbell passed the halfway point of his 557-mile Orofino-to-the-sea swim a few miles east of here Sunday, then he splashed into Arlington for a reception.

The 25-year-old swimmer attended Catholic mass at Boardman Sunday morning, started swimming from there at 12:20 p.m. and climbed out of the water at 6:10 p.m.

Campbell had a royal reception at Arlington. Dignitaries met him, and a ferryboat that crosses the Columbia River here picked him up.

"The women's auxiliary of the Veterans of Foreign Wars here presented me with some real fine opalized wood," the swimmer reported. "Then they presented me with a real nice plate with a picture of the city on it. And then we were treated to a real fine steak dinner here."

It was a happy ending for a rough day. "We had winds that were terrible, just terrible; they won't leave us alone. It just seems like the elements are out to stop us."

He added that he and his accompanying boat bucked waves six or seven feet high much of the way. Ten minutes after he started his day's journey, the boat's steering gear broke but was repaired.

The Columbia, he observed, is a different river from the Snake and Clearwater rivers he swam on the first part of his trip. "The Columbia is hard to explain—it's tricky," he said. "It's such a huge volume of water; it's like a big, gentle but ferocious creature that carries you along with it."

Campbell planned to swim to the John Day damsite, about 22 miles from Arlington, on Monday. He'll then come back to Arlington to stay over another night.

The swimmer, who hopes to reach Astoria, Ore., at the mouth of the Columbia July 28, now has swum 275 miles of his 557-mile journey. He has broken a world record, he said, by swimming 220 miles in six days. He began the swim July 2.

Marathon Swimmer Believes He's Discovered New Method

BOARDMAN, Ore. — Spencer Campbell, the Orofino-to-Astoria swimmer, Saturday claimed discovery of an "entirely new method of swimming" which he thinks will speed him down the Columbia River to the sea.

The Orofino skin-diver declined to describe in detail the "new stroke" which he "discovered by accident" Friday while swimming in the reservoir formed by McNary dam.

"It is hard to describe, and I want to check on it more anyway," he said. "It may be of some value to Navy underwater swimming teams. The best I can say now is that it is a new method of using my skin diving equipment and suit which almost entirely eliminates chafing and gives added speed. I discovered by accident how to do it, and I want to work on it more. It permits swimming at high speeds in rough water—4 miles per hour for two hours—in a relaxed way without fatigue."

Campbell discussed his discovery Saturday noon, just before he swam through the McNary dam locks and headed for Boardman, 20 miles downstream. He was to spend the night there.

He had swum against 30-mile winds Friday, leaving the water twice to wait for the winds to subside. He swam 7 hours and 40 minutes in all Friday, climbing out of the water finally at 9:20 p.m.

He started late Saturday, but with almost no wind to hamper him, and hoped to get back on a daytime swimming schedule starting Sunday.

Feels 'Very Good'

"I feel very good," he said, "although just a little tired after swimming in still water 75 miles in the last six days."

Despite delays caused by wind, motor trouble in an accompanying boat, and early chafing caused by his suit, Campbell figures he is still a day ahead of schedule in his effort to reach Astoria, Ore., by July 31.

"I figured on three days to swim through Ice Harbor dam pool and another three days for the McNary dam pool," he said. "I went through one pool in two days and through the other in one."

He said the chafing has disappeared entirely, and he is counting on his new, secret swimming method to prevent a recurrence.

CHAPTER 22

Susan

During my last year in the Air Force I spent quite a bit of my off duty time flying as a civilian pilot and I was also a check airman for our base flying club. I had my own personal small plane (a Stinson) hangared on the civilian side of the airport and spent quite a few of my weekends flying from Everett to my hometown, Lewiston.

While I was home I met a young lady at a party thrown by one of my friends. She was a vivacious little redhead, with a dynamic personality and a captivating smile. In a way, she resembled a teenage Shirley Temple. She was cute, witty, and strong-willed. She approached me at the dance and introduced herself. "I'm Susie," she said. "Susan Craig—what's your name?" "Spence Campbell," I replied. She stared at me for several long seconds through a pair of probing blue eyes. Then, without hesitation, as if a great decision had been made, she took my hand and said, "You're mine; let's dance!" Now there was a lady that didn't beat around the bush about anything, and from that moment on, I was hers.

When we returned from the Garrison Dam, I proposed to Susan

and within a few weeks we were married. We moved into a little cottage by the Spokane River on the north side of town and started our life together. I now had some time to relax and be with Susan. We watched television and did a bunch of fun things.

It was the first year that the Summer Olympics were televised and a young man by the name of Cassias Clay (now Mohamed Ali) won a gold medal for boxing for the United States. I remember telling Susan that I predicted he would someday be the world champion.

It was about four months before we started our next diving job and by then I was learning about the feast or famine aspects of professional diving. Susan and I were expecting our first child. Susan was diabetic, dependent on insulin to keep her system balanced, and she was prone to seizures if her blood sugar got too low. The seizures would come at unexpected and awkward times.

If you have never witnessed a violent seizure, it can be a traumatic experience. The victim of a seizure goes into rigid spasms, turns cyanotic and passes out, exhibiting a series of convulsive jerks. Susan and I had gone together for several years before we were married and I was used to treating her when the seizures occurred. To me, it was just a matter of allowing her to pass through the varied phases of the seizure episode and to keep her from injuring herself until she entered the relaxed or unconscious phase of the seizures.

One afternoon we were grocery shopping in a busy Safeway store when Susan grabbed me and warned me she was going to have a seizure. Individuals prone to seizures often have an aura, or warning of the seizure. As the seizure commenced, horrified shoppers stopped to stare at the spectacle. Some panicked and a couple of women almost fainted! As I bent over tending Susan who had slumped to the floor, I felt a hand on my shoulder. I looked up into the assistant store manager's panic stricken face. "What can I do?" he cried! "Don't call an ambulance; she is a diabetic," I said. "Just get me an orange or some sugar, please."

The storekeeper whirled around and disappeared. After only a few seconds he was back. "Here" he said." I was still on my knees, bent over Susan, and hadn't looked up at the manager after his hasty return. I just raised my hand, palm up, expecting to be handed an orange or a packet of sugar. Instead, I looked up to see the panicked manager pouring sugar from a 10 pound sack into my cupped, overflowing hand! When Susan recovered from the seizure and was able to walk, the assistant manager helped me steady Susan as we took her to our car.

Later when we got home I recounted the whole scenario to her. She howled with laughter when I described the look on the manager's face while he was pouring two pounds of granulated sugar into my hand. We left the Safeway store without our groceries, 3 pounds of sugar on the floor, and a shook up patronage! I felt sorry for the poor assistant manager so I went back to the store about three hours later. I bought our groceries and apologized for the inconvenience. I told him what a great job he did and paid for what was left of the sugar in the 10-pound bag.

Our next job came in January. This job involved working on the underwater metal pilings of a new railroad bridge spanning the river near an Idaho town north of Spokane. We had lots of snow that winter and the river was full of ice. We used Mark Five heavy gear with attached gloves. We wore heavy wool underwear under the diving dress and wool gloves inside the diving suit gloves. Unless the diver is moving, or the working hard, there's no way to keep the bitter cold water from slowly refrigerating the diver inside the suit.

Our work was cutting metal pilings with an oxy-arc cutting torch, which unfortunately required the diver to remain in one spot and relatively still for long periods of time. Hypothermia was a problem, and we had to be extremely careful not to get overexposed in our zeal to get the job done. The Garrison Dam job was miserably cold, but this job was twice as bad. The 15 days of diving in the icy water left me writing another chapter in my on-the-job education manual.

I didn't drink alcohol, but I found that after spending a day diving in that frigid water the only thing that could get through the body's numbing cold was about three good shots of brandy. Now I understood why Navy divers are traditionally allowed two fingers of medicinal brandy after long cold dives. Needless to say, Bill and I were happy to see this job successfully completed.

Now it was back to my honeymoon cottage and more quality time with my little, red-headed wife. At least we were in the feast part of the feast and famine routine. From mid-February through May we did some small diving jobs locally and both Susan and I took some part-time jobs to make ends meet. My thoughts of Susan were suddenly disrupted by the sound of turning props.

The Cabin Cruiser pulled away abruptly and I heard John shouting at me from our boat. I looked up to see him pointing downriver. "Looks like you have some work coming up!" he shouted. I turned to look down stream and I could see that the river was branching into channels again.

Being lowered into the icy water

CHAPTER 23

The Salvage

The river got very wide in spots, and again, we had to criss-cross the river to get into favorable channels. There was quite a welcoming committee waiting for us at Arlington, Oregon, but our arrival was almost marred by disaster. The water conditions were fairly rough with some wave action. Then some over-enthusiastic guy driving a speed-boat appeared with a boat full of people, none of whom were wearing life jackets. In spite of the notice to mariners that had been posted, our big diver's flag, and my crews' frantic attempts to wave him off, he kept coming right at us at high speed.

It was difficult for me to see him because of the three-foot waves we were in at the time, but I did hear Bill shout a warning at me. Suddenly, the bow of his boat came into view about eight feet away headed right for me. I actually had to fend off the bow of the boat with my hands to keep from getting hit and run over. As the propeller end of the boat came my way, I exhaled all the air that I could, and forced myself downward with my arms. I could see the brass propeller coming straight at me. It was no more than four feet from my head. I made a frantic twist with my upper body and my head bumped into the bottom of the boat as the whirling prop passed within one foot of my face! When I surfaced in the boat's wake, I could hear my crew yelling "strong suggestions" to the boat operator as he sped off and disappeared in the distance. At this point we added another river hazard to our growing list.

At the end of the third day we stopped at the mouth of the John Day River. There was really no where to leave the boat for the night in the Columbia, so we sailed up the John Day about 200 yards and moored the boat in a small cove along the bank of the river, just below the Bridge on Highway 84. An Oregon State Highway patrolman stopped to talk with us while we were mooring the boat. He made a call to notify Gordon Sinclair where to pick us up and said that they would have their local patrol cars check on our boat through the night as they passed through the area. We talked with the trooper awhile and told him some stories about the swim. We thanked him for his assistance and concern for our boat and then he left us to wait for our ride back to Arlington.

There had been a lot of hard swimming in the past four days and I was very tired. After dinner and some festivities sponsored by the women's auxiliary of the VFW, I went to my hotel room for some much needed sleep. I woke up to the ringing of the phone at around 2:00 a.m. I pulled it to my ear and grunted a hello. It was an Oregon State patrolman who had phoned up from the hotel lobby to tell me that our jet boat was sinking in the John Day River. I quickly dressed and woke up the crew.

We got to the river about 3:00 a.m. and found the boat still in her mooring with about four feet of her bow sticking above the surface. The State Patrol helped us find a towing service and got some emergency assistance from a marina in the area. We needed a salvage diver to help us raise the boat. Guess who?

We had scuba gear with us on the trip and fortunately we had taken it back to the hotel with us. With the help of the State Patrol, a good-natured tow truck driver, and a marina owner who brought a truck and trailer to pick up the boat, we got it floating again. Now we were able to start the salvage operations.

We would have to rig a cable from the tow truck on the bridge above so we could lift the back of the boat above the surface and pump out the water. By 5:30 the sun was up, and so was the boat. I had made a temporary patch of the area where the sharp rocks had chaffed through the fiberglass hull causing her to sink. Unknown to us, the river level had dropped about three feet. The drop in water level was enough to put the *No-Name* on the rocks at the mooring site.

Fortunately, there was a boat launching ramp on the opposite side of the river, just below the bridge. We were able to get the boat on the trailer provided by the marina owner and send it off for repairs. It had definitely been a long night. I was cold and really needed to warm up and get some rest. I swam 21 miles the day before, been up most of the night, and spent nearly two hours underwater rigging a boat lift and putting a temporary patch on the hull of the *No-Name*. I started to feel like a commercial diver again!

My crew took me back to Arlington for some breakfast and a couple of hours of rest while we contemplated our new dilemma. We had no boat, I had to try to make some river mileage, and Devil's Doorway was in the next stretch of river. We were becoming very frustrated when the owner of the marina called the hotel to tell us that they were working on the boat and one of his close friends had volunteered himself and his 20-foot boat to escort us down the river until we could get the *No-Name* repaired. That was another example of the phenomenal support we got from everyone along the way.

I felt bad for King Cole who had to call his boss, Floyd Harvey, and tell him the "wonderful" news about the *No-Name*. It was enough that Floyd might suffer financial loss on the boat's earning potential while it was tied up on my adventure, but now, there would be damage and repairs. I thought Floyd would be upset and want the boat returned to his operation after it was fixed, but to my complete surprise, he told King to have the marina owner contact him and do whatever it took to get the boat running and back in the river with me.

Our volunteer safety boat, and its cordial skipper, Frank, met us about 10 a.m. at the John Day River. King, John, Bill and I got aboard and we sailed out into the middle of the river, where I entered the water to begin the day's swim. After about five hours of swimming in fairly smooth, steady current downstream, King announced that we were approaching "Devil's Doorway" at "Hell's Gate".

We passed through the entrance of the "doorway," carried by a fairly fast current and, again, I could feel strange undercurrents on my legs and fins. We entered a narrow channel bordered by vertical rock walls and then we came around a sharp bend where the river seemed to run straight ahead into another vertical rock wall. The current was pretty fast and as we approached, back surge from all the water hitting the wall forced us away from it and propelled us at nearly right angles through another narrow passage. It seemed as if we were going through a series of small vertical rock wall channels. The water looked turbulent, but really wasn't bad to swim through.

It was a fairly short trip through the Devil's Doorway. And fortunately, it was not the monster we had expected. After the anticipated excitement of the "doorway," there was just a lot of monotonous swimming. After some of the excitement we had in the Snake River I was perfectly satisfied with monotonous.

After the "doorway", I was really resting. I was floating on my back, staring up into the blue summer sky, when a small plane swooped low over the river and circled over us several times. The sight of the small plane sent my thoughts back in time to when I joined the Air Force. I wanted to be a fighter pilot. The plane made a few more passes and then flew off out of sight. Now, there was just blue sky with a few lazy white clouds.

CHAPTER 24

Wild Blue Yonder

It was June 1954. Only about three weeks had elapsed since graduation when Roy, Charlie, and I decided to join the Air Force. I was only 17 and wouldn't be 18 until September so my dad had to sign for me. We went to Spokane for our induction physical, which we all passed with flying colors. Then we went back to Lewiston to wait our acceptance and induction orders.

Five days before we got our orders, Charlie fell and broke his leg! He was forced to stay home to recuperate while Roy and I shipped out. We arrived by bus at Lackland Air Force Base, San Antonio, Texas on the sixth of July. Our bus rolled in at dusk, and even though the sun was setting, it was still miserably hot. After we got off the bus we checked in and were turned over to our training instructor, (T.I.). Roy and I were separated into different flights as they called them.

We were all very tired, very hot, and very thirsty. As we stumbled out of the orientation building and assembled into somewhat of a formation, we were told by our new T.I., Mr. Bradford, how happy he was to see us and what a wonderful and rewarding experience we were all about to have.

His acceptance speech went something like this: "Greetings rainbows (rainbows were new recruits, who were still in civilian clothes of varying colors). For the next three months, you are mine. I am your mother and your father! You have no other life other than the US Air Force. You may consider yourself lower than whale excrement and cannot possibly be worth anything to anyone in your present state. I will change that! Looking at you now it seems like an impossible task, but in spite of the odds against me, I will make military men of you. I will do that and in doing so, no doubt make your lives miserable for the next 90 days. Welcome to Fight 317 of the United States Air Force. Now pick up your bags and follow me."

Encouraged by our welcome speech we marched along to our squadron barracks. There were about 50 of us in Flight 317 and once we reached the barracks we were divided into groups of 12. The groups were then taken into a small room, stood at attention, and harassed for about half an hour that seemed like an eternity. The T. I. and his assistants would interrogate each one of us and ask us questions, for which we would consistently give unsatisfactory answers. With each unsatisfactory answer, there was a consequence: push-ups, squats, or something. Occasionally, someone would give a really stupid answer, or the T. I. would say something about someone's posture. "What are you doing all hunched over like a monkey, making love to a football?" (Nicer version). Hardly anyone could resist laughing and that was a serious mistake.

The evening progressed, and finally after the hazing the whole flight was assembled on the bottom floor of the barracks. The one water fountain, which was off-limits when we arrived, was now open to us. We were all dying of thirst and we lined up to get a drink. Our T.I. told us we could have a drink, but we had to count off each swallow! After the first 10 men had taken their drink, the rest of us threatened to kill anyone who took more than three swallows! The evening took far too long.

We were told to get undressed and get into our temporarily assigned bunks. Our T.I. then proclaimed, " lights out and no talking!" He told us all to get plenty of sleep because reveille came
rather early. He said that the Air Force had a busy day of welcoming ceremonies planned for us, starting at 4:30 a.m. When I finally
closed my eyes that night, I seriously contemplated the wisdom of
my choice of activities for the next four years.

After all the shots, a very short haircut, our issue of Air Force
uniforms, and several weeks of constant abuse, we got used to the
chow and the marching. Little by little, we were molded into a uni-
fied group of military men. Now, some people might think that
Air Force basic training is pansy stuff compared with the Army, or
Marine boot camp, but remember this was 1954. The U.S. Air Force
was only a few years old. Air Force basic was still Army boot camp,
at least, it sure felt like it!

In the weeks that followed, we begin to look, act, and think like
military men. After weapons training, we had our bivouac. (a no
fun, military camping trip). We stayed in small pup tents out in the
field for one week. The temperature in San Antonio was 120°. This
was when I received the homemade fudge I had requested in a letter to my stepmother. Four pie plate tins of wonderful, homemade
Idaho fudge arrived at evening mail call. As I opened the package
it started melting in the heat; what a time to get my fudge! I just
handed one plate to the lead tent in the first three rows of flights
and told them to enjoy. I saved one tin for our flight. I cut a couple
of chunks from the fudge for myself and then passed the tin down
our row of tents.

The 11 weeks of basic training went by fast. Glorious was the
day that we earned our first stripe. I had it sewed on two of my
shirts within one hour of receiving the rank. We had about four
days processing out from basic training and waiting to receive our
orders to our first Air Force career training bases.

In the two remaining days I was asked to help our training

instructor pick up a new group of rainbows and indoctrinate them. At that moment, I came face-to-face with the sadistic side of my nature. As much as I hated what was done to me on the first two days of boot camp, I could hardly wait to be the tormentor instead of the "tormentee." I was the perfect choice for Mr. Bradford. For two days, I struck fear and trepidation into the hearts of 50 men. I used a loud, authoritative sounding voice and brandished a huge single stripe on my sleeve. It was a majestic experience!

I spent the next year at Lowry Air Force Base in Denver, Colorado where I was trained as a fire control technician. My job was to troubleshoot and repair the electronic systems that fire and guide air-to-air missiles that are carried by all-weather, fighter/interceptor aircraft assigned to the Air Defense command. The Cold War with Russia was heating up rapidly and at that time my Air Force career field was critical to our nation's defense. The training at Lowry took almost a year and by then I had two stripes.

My first duty assignment was at McCord Air Force Base in Tacoma, Washington. I was assigned to the 318th fighter interceptor squadron, but first, I would get a well-earned 30-day leave to go back to Shangri-La.

Since I really wanted to be a pilot in the Air Force, but didn't have the academic qualifications at that time, I did the next best thing. I spent most of my 30-day leave at Hillcrest Airport learning to fly as a civilian pilot.

My flight instructor was one of the pilots that flew the Stearman biplane crop-dusters for Hillcrest Aircraft Co.

I took my primary training in a small tandem, two-place, tail-wheel airplane called an "Aeronica Champ." My instructor was a great guy, very firm, with a great personality, and a good sense of humor. I'm so thankful that I learned to fly stick and rudder from John. He was a demanding instructor, and a real pilot's pilot. I took to the training like a bird to flight (no pun intended) Even though I made some mistakes, I loved every minute of it! When we did our forced landing training, John wasn't satisfied until I was three feet above the stubble of a wheat field before he would give me a pass.

We were six days into my training; I had logged a whopping total of five hours and 55 minutes of dual instruction. After several takeoffs and landings, John asked me to taxi over to the apron in front of the hangar and stop.

I thought the session was over, but John said to keep it running. He got out of the back seat, and stood on the apron. He leaned into the front cockpit area and said, "Go fly the pattern and make three takeoffs and landings to a full stop, then come back here." I couldn't believe he was going to allow me to solo. "John", I said, "I botched up two of those five landings we just practiced." He looked at me and said, "Yes, you did, but you also did the right things to recover. I don't worry about students who make mistakes and know how to recover. I worry about students that don't seem to make any mistakes. Now, leave the nest and fly."

He closed up the cockpit doors and backed away from the airplane. I added some throttle and the little yellow and orange Champ started moving off the apron onto the taxiway. I was excited to solo, but I was also nervous. My mind raced through the various elements of the coming flight. I got to the end of the taxiway and pulled over into the pre-takeoff area.

Methodically, I went through all of the pre-takeoff checks, carefully checked the pattern for traffic, and taxied out onto the runway. I was accustomed to John's reassuring voice coaching me before the takeoff roll, but this time there was no voice. A quick glance over my shoulder verified that the back seat was empty. It was now time to become a pilot.

The three takeoffs and landings were uneventful, but I didn't like the second approach, so I decided to go around again and there were no further problems. After my last landing, I taxied to the ramp and shut down by John who was waiting with a huge grin and a pair of scissors to cut off my T-shirt. That was the custom for "first solo" student pilots.

The first major flight adventure came just one week after my first solo flight. I was now a seasoned pilot with a grand total of eight and a half hours of flying time. It was at the Clarkston Airport, (which no longer exists), but used to be located alongside and parallel to the Snake River. It was a gravel runway, and a good place for a student to practice because there wasn't much traffic. My instructor was doing some work in Clarkston that day. He told me to meet him at the Clarkston airport for my flight lesson.

When I arrived, he still had some work to finish so he said to take the plane and go practice some takeoffs and landings. This would be my third solo flight, and I was excited to do more solo flights. It was a warm summer afternoon and the winds were light and pretty much straight down the runway. It seemed like a perfect day to fly.

I had been in the air practicing for about 30 minutes, and was just about to turn and lineup with the runway for a landing when the aircraft didn't seem to be responding to my control inputs. Suddenly I was aware of very heavy wind gusts, making it tough to control the plane. I looked ahead and saw a huge dust storm coming up the river canyon right at me. About that same time John came running out onto the runway and waved me off from my attempt to land. He was waving his arms and pointing in the direction of the Lewiston airport. I figured he wanted me to go to Hillcrest where I would have a more favorable runway direction for the high gusty winds.

As I turned the little Champ toward the Lewiston airport, I saw John run and jump into his pickup truck. It was about 8 miles from the Clarkston airport to Hillcrest and it seemed like only a few minutes after I got over the Lewiston airport that John's pickup pulled into the parking lot. It was then that I noticed one small airplane that had been blown over on its back, and two others that were blown up against other aircraft. The situation did not look encouraging!

A few minutes after John disappeared into the hangar, he and three men came running out onto the apron and headed toward the end of one of the runways. I was in the pattern, and could see John motioning me to continue circling and wait. I made a couple of wild, irregular circuits of the traffic pattern as the wind seemed to intensify and hammer the small plane unmercifully.

By now, John and the other men had positioned themselves near the touchdown area of one of the runways. John pointed to the touchdown area and motioned for me to land on that runway. Fortunately, the wind had stopped its wild gusting, but was still howling at about 60 miles an hour. My landing speed would be 50 to 60 miles an hour through the air and the wind would be forcing me back at 60 miles an hour. As silly as it sounds, my speed over the ground would be zero. With full power, the little plane would only do about 85 to 90 miles an hour—tops.

I circled around the field and lined up with the runway John had pointed out. He and the others were standing near the end of the runway. I caught a couple of pretty bad gusts on the decent, but as I got within 100 feet of the runway the wind was very strong, but steady on the nose.

As I flew over the end of the runway, my 15 mph speed over the ground made me feel like I was flying a helicopter instead of an airplane. I did see John, who was about 40 yards down the runway and off to one side, motioning me to keep the power up on the landing. I was going to do that anyway, because if I didn't I would start flying backwards!

There was a couple of tense moments when a big gust hit me as I was about 10 feet above the runway, but I compensated quickly with the stick and rudder, and got it back under control before it wobbled its way onto the runway. During the last uncomfortable drop to the asphalt, I sort of gritted my teeth and turned over the final touchdown to God and St. Michael. Both of them came through for me and as the little red and yellow Champ bounced onto the runway. Men appeared on both sides of the airplane and grabbed the wing struts as I backed down the power.

John was alongside now, shouting at me to keep some power on and steer the airplane across the smooth grass toward the hangar. As we got to the ramp near the hangar, one of the men ran ahead and opened the hangar door. The other men and John kept hold of the plane. As we started into the hangar, John signaled me to kill the engine. I pulled back the throttle and cut the ignition. The noise of the engine faded into the howling of the wind. The men quickly pushed the airplane and me into the hangar and closed the doors. John leaned inside the cockpit and said, "Good job. You did a great job landing this thing in that wind and turbulence! Come on into the lounge and let me buy you a cup of coffee." He turned and walked off into the pilot's lounge.

I sat there for a few minutes staring at the instrument panel; only then did the full realization hit me that life was finite, and I had been very lucky. There went life number three! When I got into the lounge, all the pilots, instructors, and maintenance guys grinned at me, and gave me a "thumbs up." Even though my hand was still shaking when I filled out my logbook, I felt like real pilot!

A couple of days later, I was back flying again. I had about 25 hours logged by the time my leave was up and I had to go to my duty station at McCord Air Force Base in Tacoma, Washington.

I reported for duty with the 318th fighter interceptor squadron. The F-86 D all weather interceptor at McChord was using the E-4 fire control system to control its missiles and I was looking forward to being a technician working on fighter planes. During the time I was with the 318th, I kept myself occupied in my off-duty hours by practicing archery. I even organized a base archery club.

During the early summer of 1956, I read a book titled, The Blue Continent. The book made such an impression on me that I felt I had to learn how to scuba dive, but there were no scuba training programs in the Tacoma area at that time. A local downtown hardware store had some scuba equipment for sale so I bought an air tank, a regulator, fins, mask, snorkel and a weight belt. I bought a diving suit through a *Skin Diver* Magazine ad; now all I had to do was to learn how to dive.

In the box with my "Healthways" regulator was a small green and white manual titled, *Underwater Safety* written by E. R. Cross. By reading the manual and following its instruction carefully, I was able to teach myself how to scuba dive. I practiced in American Lake and in Puget Sound beneath the Steilacoom ferry dock. I made some mistakes, but with the help of Mr. Cross, and his manual, I didn't drown! A year later, I would take a formal certification course in Los Angeles.

I spent a year with the 318th squadron, and then I applied for a new missile systems school. I had to extend my enlistment for several months and take an exam to qualify for the training. I passed the test, was accepted, and spent the next year in school at Hughes Aircraft Co. in Culver City, a suburb of Los Angeles.

The training was classified top-secret and we lived like civilians in apartments, or rented houses. We were not allowed to talk about our training with anyone outside the class under the threat of imprisonment. The fighter missile system that we studied would control the launch and guidance of the first air-to-air atomic missile.

The school was very intense, and all of our instructors had their masters or Ph.D.'s in mathematics, electronics, or physics. We went to school from 7:00 a.m. to 3:30 p.m., and it was highly technical training. Being top-secret, there was no homework—both a good thing and a bad thing. Fortunately, they did give us some time to study in school. During the training, which covered everything from complex electronics to basic nuclear physics, I rekindled my high school interest in science. I was still interested in space and rockets, but I began to develop a fascination about human physiology and medical science.

During my off school hours I spent time working on my private pilot's license and passed my check ride in June 1957. I was now a licensed private pilot. I also spent some spare time reading library books on scientific subjects and making some rather awkward attempts at dating women. At that stage of my life I just didn't seem to have the need for girlfriends, not that I didn't appreciate the opposite sex, I just found other things more important to me.

For about six months, I lived in an apartment complex right across the street from the main entrance of MGM Studios. Sometimes I would watch the limos and cars entering and leaving the studios to see if I could recognize any of the big stars. I think I saw a few. Because of my amateur acting experience I couldn't help but fantasize about being discovered and becoming a big star myself, but it never happened! Oh well, Hollywood's loss!

The year long training went by quickly and after a 30-day leave it was on to my new duty assignment at Paine Air Force Base in Everett, Washington. Everett is a city about 30 miles north of Seattle. It was an Air Defense command base on a joint military/civilian airport. I was assigned to the 326th fighter interceptor squadron. Our planes were Northrop F-89-J Scorpions. These were twin engine, all-weather interceptors that would carry the United States first air-to-air nuclear missiles (basically, a flying 1.5 kiloton atomic bomb!) During 1958 and 1959, we were well into the hot part of the Cold War, and because of the Russian threat, the coastal areas of the United States bristled with defense.

The Scorpion also carried radar guided and infrared seeking missiles as part of its weaponry. Because the Scorpion could not fly as high as the Russian bombers they sought to destroy, they had to climb up toward the bombers in what was called a "snap up maneuver" and fire the missile up toward the bomber fleet as the aircraft neared a stall. The nuclear explosion from the Genie missile would create a one half-mile fireball. This would destroy some bombers and incapacitate others. The problem for the fighter that launched the nuclear missile was to get far enough away from the blast after the launch to avoid being destroyed. There was serious speculation that the Scorpion could not escape the blast.

The flight teams took turns pulling alert duty. They lived in a fire station-like building at the end of the runway, complete with brass poles and openings to allow them to slide down from their second-floor bunkroom to the hangar deck below. Four fighters were always primed and ready for launch at a moment's notice.

Sometimes I pulled alert hangar duty and would get to spend several days with pilot crews and support staff. It was not uncommon that at least three times in four days there would be a scramble on unidentified targets, or a tactical action by Air Defense command to test the airplanes, pilots, and crew readiness. Of necessity, they never told the pilots it was just a drill, and often those pilots and radar observers would streak off into day or night to intercept targets that were presumed hostile.

Most of the time the fighter crews would not know if they were on the front line of an actual air war until the targets were identified as friendly, or the brass running the exercise called them back. Some of those pilots lived for years under the Sword of Damocles, and as far as I'm concerned, they never got the credit they deserved. I just pray that we will always find men like them to serve our country.

CHAPTER 25

The Tunnels

It was strange that on such a demanding challenge as the river swim, I would have such vivid memories from earlier years and I wondered if Lewis and Clark had reminisced about their early lives while traveling the river. Maybe there was some spirit of recollections that haunted the route forcing challengers to reflect on their past.

The wind began picking up, and I could feel the surface of the river start to roll. I glanced up from the grey depths at my crew in the safety boat. My brother Bill must have sensed that I could use some company. He put on his hood, fins, and mask and jumped in the river to swim along with me for several miles. Both John and Bill swam a lot of miles on the trip.

Strong winds came up in the afternoon and made it rough and miserable for the swim through the backwaters of the Dalles Dam. They issue small craft warnings for the Columbia River and I know from experience why they do! We arrived at the dam just as it was getting dark, and were met by a small welcoming committee of town dignitaries from The Dalles, Oregon. They had planned a small

River Runner Approaching Dalles Dam

ARLINGTON, Ore. — Spencer Campbell, who made another 21 miles Monday on his 557-mile swim from Orofino to the sea, said he again will turn to an evening swim Tuesday night to "try to get away from the wind."

He said he plans to make 20 miles more Tuesday to The Dalles Dam.

He has "battled ferocious winds all the way from McNary reservoir," he said, adding: "It couldn't be worse."

"Local people say it is ridiculous for this time of year. It's very cold for the time of year. It should be over 100 degrees but it's been in the 70s."

However, he noted he's still beating his planned 16 miles a day after leaving McNary Dam. His successive daily swims have been 22, 26 and 21 miles. He's also three days ahead of his schedule now.

Reaches River

He left Arlington Monday morning at 11:45 and went the 21 miles to the John Day River which is a mile above the John Day damsite. He left the water at 5:45 p.m. and returned to Arlington for the night. A considerable delegation saw him off Monday, including city officials.

Campbell figures to hit the water again about the time the wind begins dying down around 6:30 p.m. Tuesday.

He said he "hit a few whirlpools" Monday and "a few very bad rapids."

"It's a very wicked river," he said. "It's a good river not to get too far out into. You stay close to shore so you can get back in safely."

But he added:

"I feel fine. Still feel great and I'm going all the way."

■ ■

celebration for the next morning when we were scheduled to go through the locks at the dam.

That evening we got the *No-Name* back. We thanked Frank, our interim skipper for his help and the use of his boat and we made him an official member of the river swim team. During the next two days, I swam downriver to White Salmon, then onto the Bonneville Dam. During the second day, the afternoon winds were ferocious so we opted to wait until night for the winds to die down before I attempted to swim the expanse of Lake-like reservoir behind the Bonneville Dam. It was just too rough on the boat crew and me to be out on the river trying to swim in those conditions!

Again we found it necessary to swim at night. The darkness and the black water seemed to make the swim harder and the night lasted far too long. After five or six hours, I felt like I had been swimming forever. We finally arrived about one half mile upstream from the dam at around 3:00 in the morning. It was too late and too early to go anywhere, so we just stretched out on the deck of the boat and slept until daylight. After a couple hours of rest, we got up and took the boat to a dock at the reservoir, where we contacted some of the personnel from the dam. They made a couple of phone calls for us and located our welcoming committee.

We were able to rest for a couple more hours before we had to enter the locks. I stayed by the side of the *No-Name* as the water was being lowered. There were only a few boats in the lock. Looking around the concrete structure, and listening to the pulsating sounds coming through the water, took me back to the Hungry Horse Dam and my inspection dives in the draft tubes.

In mid June of 1960 Bill called and said we had won the bid on the Hungry Horse Dam in Montana, and we would need to get our gear ready for the job. That was music to my ears and my heart was happy, for I was again a working deep-sea diver. It took about 10 days to organize the equipment and load the truck for the trip to Hungry Horse. Bill and I would be the only ones going and I would be the only diver on this job.

I was excited about the new diving job, but leery about leaving Susan, who was four months pregnant. Pregnancies could be trouble for severe diabetics. Fortunately, Susan's parents, Doc and Jean Craig, were living in Spokane and could look after her while I was gone. The Craigs were wonderful people who were very supportive of my diving career. They had lived with Susan's chronic diabetic condition since she was five years old. Without their help I wouldn't have been able to go to distant diving jobs for weeks at a time.

The drive to Hungry Horse, Montana was another adventure in good eating. Bill was in rare form as we stopped at various restaurants along the way. We arrived at Hungry Horse Dam on Friday. This dam was operated and managed by the U.S. Bureau of Reclamation. It was a magnificent structure, trapping and storing several hundred feet of water between two steep canyon walls. It was a "high head" dam, referring to the depth of water behind the reservoir, which was several hundred feet deep.

The Flathead River filled the huge mountain reservoir and water deep in the reservoir was channeled through the dam to turn the turbines that made electrical power. The water flowing out of the draft tubes was about 60 feet deep. It was very clear and the temperature was not much above freezing.

This dam was also experiencing draft tube gate leaks and the engineers could not pump out the water for dry inspections. My first dives were made in the tailrace to inspect the draft tube gates. The tailrace is usually very turbulent because several units are kept running to provide electricity. The discharge of water coming from the draft tube tunnels is very strong, and it would be impossible for a diver to work near the flow of a running unit. A diver would be able to work only on units that have been shut down.

Prior to diving operations, the Diving Supervisor and the Operating Engineers conduct a safety lockout inspection of all controls that operate critical valves or gates. Controls operated at the wrong time could release tons of water on a diver working in the draft tube area, or suck the diver into the intakes on the reservoir side of the dam.

Mechanical locks and warning signs are used to secure critical valves to ensure the diver's safety. They warn all operating personnel at the dam when diving operations are in progress. Critical controls cannot be operated without a key and an authorization from both the Chief Engineer and the Diving Supervisor.

When a diver is 180 feet below the surface, within two to three feet of an intake on the upstream side of the dam, it is comforting to know that safeguards are in place that would prevent someone from accidentally opening a valve that could cause the diver to be sucked into the intake. If that were to happen the diver would make a rapid, and unintentional trip, through the dam's water system. Unfortunately, he would never live to tell about it. After our meeting with the Chief Engineer, we moved our gear onto the dive site and studied some engineering drawings. Now we were ready to secure our operations until Monday morning when the diving job was scheduled to begin.

Over the weekend we did some sightseeing in the local area. In our wanderings we visited the studios of Ace Powell and his wife. Ace Powell was a well-known local artist specializing in portraits and scenes of the Blackfoot Indian tribe. They were fascinated by our diving work and we were fascinated by their artwork. Over the four weeks of the diving job, we got to know Ace and his wife quite well. We were able to get them onto the job site one day to watch the diving operations and they had Bill and I over to their place for dinner one evening.

The weather was perfect, sunny, and warm. The cold clear water of the tailrace was great for diving. Visibility in the slow-moving water away from the running generators was fantastic. What a pleasure it was to be able to actually see what you were working on. Again, we had to use the boom truck and chain stage to lower the diver over the backside of the dam to the water about 60 feet below.

It was another 60 feet down to the bottom to the concrete apron that projects from the draft tube tunnels a few yards and then blends into the natural river bottom. The river bottom downstream from the draft tubes consisted of medium-size to fairly large boulders and smaller rocks. The water was clear enough that I could see about 100 feet downstream. There were huge trout swimming about and I'm sure the ones I was seeing were the big ones that always got away.

On our initial inspections we discovered that the "Ground Mat" was in need of serious repair. This is a web of large copper cable stretching across the bottom of the tailrace that provides electrical grounding for the dam and helps protect the dam during lightning storms. We also found several steel gate guides. These are steel beams that help position the huge draft tube gates as they are lowered into place to seal off the draft tubes. They had been sheared off, and we found them 30 to 40 feet downstream lying on the bottom. The loss of these gate guides could cause the gates to bind as they were lowered into place. Binding of the gates would cause them to seal improperly and allow leakage into the draft tubes.

Discovery of the broken gate guides created a new diving task of repairing and reinstalling them. This work involved rigging a unique diver work platform and some tricky drilling with a heavy air operated underwater drill. I learned a lot on this job from Bill who was a master of rigging and working with machinery and tools.

Diving work to repair and reinstall the gate guides was moving along smoothly, but the engineers were still having trouble with major leaks on two of the units. They were able to lower the water inside the tubes to just below an access hatch, which was directly below the huge turbine blades that are turned by the water. The 20-foot diameter tube below the "scroll case," as it is called, drops about 30 feet to the bottom where it divides into three draft tube tunnels. The draft tube tunnels are about 15 feet by 15 feet square and it is about 135 feet through the tunnels from the scroll case area to the draft tube gates. The water level was about 10 feet below the access hatch and the water was about 20 feet deep down to the floor of the draft tube tunnels.

The engineers could get access to the scroll case through the hatch, but because of the leakage, could not descend into the draft tube tunnels. The engineers decided that a diver should inspect the draft tubes of the flooded units for signs of structural damage. Bill informed me that I would be that diver. The idea of penetrating those submerged pitch-black tunnels, with no access to the surface except 135 feet horizontally and then 20 feet vertically, was both challenging and intimidating.

Two days later we finished repairing and installing the gate guides. Now it was time for the inside inspections. We couldn't get a diver in Mark-Five deep-sea gear through the 28-inch hatch opening, so we elected to do the dive in a neoprene wet suit. The diving equipment that we chose was a simple triangular shaped rubber mask, called a "Desco mask," and sometimes referred to as Jack Brown "equipment."

The air is delivered through a small diameter hose leading from the mask up to an air supply source on the surface. Airflow to the mask is controlled with a small hand operated valve located on the bottom side of the mask. The diver wears a harness and a weight belt. The lifeline and air hose umbilical is securely attached to the diver's harness to prevent any strain on the umbilical from pulling off the diver's mask while he is underwater.

Modern commercial divers would be able to make this dive in much safer equipment, but it did not exist in 1959. The only equipment we had available for commercial diving then was various types of heavy helmets, a few variations of full-face mask units similar to the Desco and Scuba (self-contained under water breathing apparatus). The safest alternative to Mark Five equipment for this dive was the Desco line tended equipment.

We set up a staging area in the concrete hallway next to the "scroll-case" access hatch. I dressed in for the first dive into the tunnels, and Bill hooked up an underwater light for me to use on the dive. It was a powerful Navy deep sea diving light with a long cable using electrical power from the surface.

I put on the harness and weight belt and we secured the lifeline and air hose to the harness. Next, I placed the Desco mask over my face, and adjusted and tightened the five straps holding the mask in place on my head. I started the air flowing by adjusting the valve on the side of the mask. Then I got up from the dressing stool and walked with Bill over to the access hatch. Even with the lightweight diving gear it was a relatively small opening to pass through without snagging something.

Once through the access hatch, I positioned myself on the vertical hanging ladder inside the scroll case and started to climb down to the water, which was about 10 feet below the hatch. The engineers had rigged an electric light inside the huge scroll case, and it cast an adequate, but eerie light on the surface of the water below me.

The water was crystal clear, and even with only the one bulb

Entering the hatch for dives in the Hungry Horse Draft Tube Tunnels

light source, I could see through the water down to the concrete floor. I climbed down and stood on the bottom rung of the ladder submerged up to my shoulders. As always, water leaked into various areas of the wet suit and provided a few moments of discomfort while it trickled down to parts of my body that I probably shouldn't mention! The wet suit traps a layer of water against the body and the water doesn't circulate so the heat from the diver's body warms up the water and provides insulation and warmth—at least that's the way it's supposed to work in theory. Fortunately, I had on thick neoprene gloves to keep my hands from freezing in the cold water.

While standing at the base of the ladder waiting to start the dive, I looked up and around the inside of the large confining cylinder of the "scroll case." About 20 feet above was the huge turbine unit that turns the electrical generator. For a few seconds I had mental flash of what would happen if the upstream intake gate were accidentally opened. I chastised myself for thinking about that kind of thing now; besides, there was nothing I could do if it did happen.

I refocused my thoughts on the job, adjusted the airflow to the mask, and started my descent to the bottom. Landing on the concrete floor of the scroll case, I slipped my feet into a large pair of fins. Because my buoyancy allowed me to swim, I could propel myself with the fins, and in essence, swim like a scuba diver. I wouldn't be quite as free, however, because I was dragging my long umbilical and a power cord for my underwater light.

After adjusting my air and buoyancy, I turned toward the entrance of the big draft tube tunnels. I looked at the three large openings leading toward the back of the dam and the draft tube gates. The beam from my light penetrated into the first of the concrete tunnels I was to inspect. The light illuminated the tunnel for about 30 feet and then was absorbed by the blackness beyond. I knew that once I penetrated the tunnel very far, the risk of not being able to reach surface in an emergency would increase with every foot I traveled.

I entered the first of the long tunnels and turned my thoughts to inspecting the concrete for signs of damage. I looked for areas that might be eroding because of the forces of the fast flowing water when the unit was operating. The water was gin clear, and the temperature was around 37 degrees. It seemed much colder than the tailrace water outside the tunnels. I moved further into the draft tube, and I could feel resistance from the light cord and the umbilical as I pulled them with me into the tunnel. When I was about 40 feet from the gate I could see it in my light. I also felt a significant current flowing against me coming from the gate. When I was within 30 feet I could see the gate clearly. The current was quite strong and I was having difficulty swimming against it.

I discovered that the current was mainly on the right side of the 15 ft. wide draft tube so I moved over to the left side where the current was minimal and continued toward the gate. When I got within 6 feet, I realized that the current and turbulence was coming from the bottom of the gate. It appeared that the gate might be raised slightly off the bottom at one end. By swimming seven to eight feet above the bottom I could get to the gate without being pushed back by the turbulence and current. I reasoned that the huge seven ton gate might be in a bind and cocked at the bottom, or possibly resting on a rock.

There was a big difference between the water pressure outside the gate and the pressure inside the draft tube and it was creating a large flow of water under the gate into the partly sealed draft tube. The next few minutes of this dive would teach me one of the harsh lessons, reserved especially for young, eager, bulletproof deep-sea divers. In my zeal to discover the cause of the problem, I slowly worked my way to the bottom of the gate. I was trying to get close enough to look under the gate with my light to see if I could detect any debris or obstruction.

When I neared the bottom of the gate, the water flow was quite strong and I had to struggle against the current and turbulence to keep from being pushed back. At this point I decided to take a lunge toward the bottom to get a quick look under the gate. I got my head within 6 inches of the concrete floor and turned my face toward the flow. A sudden blast of current surged past my head lifting the Desco mask off my face. Immediately, another blast of water pushed the mask up onto my forehead and instinctively, I released my grip on the gate and the underwater light and grabbed for the mask with both hands to keep from losing it completely.

Too late!! One more quick blast of current, and the mask was gone before I could get my hands on it! Ice-cold water flooded my face and my vision was reduced to a blur. I could see only a faint glow from the diving light, which had been blown off into the distance by the current. My immediate problem was locating the air hose clamped to my diving harness and following the three-foot section of hose to my mask, and its life giving air. During the turmoil of losing the mask, I sank to the floor of the draft tube and was bouncing off the bottom in the current and turbulence, desperately struggling to regain the mask and air supply.

Just as I was reeling in the hose with my mask at the end, the diving light, which was blown away by the current, must have banged against the side of the concrete tunnel. The impact was enough to damage the bulb. Instantly I was immersed in total darkness! By this time, I had the mask in my hands and had placed it over my face. I performed the emergency retrieval maneuver I had practiced many times in diving school, only this was no drill! It took a few seconds, but the water was gone and I was able to breathe again. I was totally disoriented, floating somewhere between the ceiling and the floor of the draft tube. The effect of the extremely cold water, the darkness, and lack of spatial orientation made me feel dizzy, like I might be losing consciousness. My heavily gloved hands made it difficult to get the web of mask straps over my head and before I could get the mask secured, another wave of dizziness hit me and I was afraid I would pass out. I was still holding the mask in place with my hands, and I knew if I passed out, I would lose the mask again and drown. The phrase "emergency situation" took on a whole new meaning right then. Holding the mask in place with one hand, I grasped the lifeline and air hose leading up to my tender.

Thank God Bill was a good tender as well as a good diving supervisor. When I was blown back from the gate, Bill had picked up the slack in the diving hose. Tenders are taught to keep tension on the diving umbilical so they can feel the diver working and maintain a proper tension for line pull signals. I could feel the tension and quickly gave a series of pulls, signaling an emergency! Immediately, I could feel a surging strain on the umbilical pulling me out of the tunnel toward the scroll case.

The motion of being pulled toward the entrance made me very

dizzy and again I felt like I was losing consciousness. I was losing my grip on the mask and felt it slipping way from my face.

I must have retained the mask long enough to reach the scroll case before I blacked out. All I remember was entering a fuzzy darkness. In the distance I could see a faint glow of light. The light came toward me growing brighter and brighter. I remember thinking, "Ok, this is it. Next stop St. Peter's Golden Gate." The light grew brighter, and formed a fuzzy image that focused itself into a light bulb. It was the light bulb hanging inside the scroll case by the ladder. Slowly, I realized I was at the surface and reached out and grabbed a ladder rung.

My awareness slowly returned and I felt a free-flowing stream of air bubbling up from my diving mask. It was dangling below me from the hose attached to my harness. Instinctively I pulled it up and shut off the valve. When I looked up the ladder, I was relieved to see Bill Harris and not St. Peter! Bill had a tight strain on the umbilical holding me plumb against the ladder at the surface. His face was contorted into a look of great concern. "What happened?" he asked. I wanted to blurt out that I had almost drowned, but for some reason I was compelled to think about the situation before answering, then I said, "My light is broken and it's pitch black in those tunnels." Bill acknowledged with a frown and a nod, and started pulling up the light cord.

While Bill was repairing the light, I had about 15 minutes to consider my options. My last dive could have had fatal consequences, and I was sort of in residual shock. I was now faced with the choice of quitting the dive, and telling Bill what really happened or going back into the tunnels.

All divers know they can terminate a dive at any time if they are incapacitated or their safety is being compromised. Bill Harris was the kind of supervisor who would always back his diver's decision regarding safety. I could have easily climbed up the ladder and told Bill that I needed a timeout, but another channel of reasoning was telling me that if I felt up to it physically, I should face my fears and go back in the tunnels. By the time Bill reappeared in the hatch with the underwater light I had made up my mind to continue the inspection.

Bill lowered the light to me, and once again I put on the Desco mask. I pulled the straps over my head and tightened them (really tight, this time). Then I slowly submerged to the floor of the scroll case. I stood on the bottom and adjusted my airflow, while assessing my physical and mental condition to continue. The three dark tunnel openings stood waiting for me. I pointed the light into the middle tunnel, and without further hesitation, started swimming down its long dark length.

During my swim down the tunnel, I focused my complete attention on the walls of the draft tube looking for signs of concrete damage. This time I approached this draft tube gate with a lot more caution! There was some current and turbulence, but it was minimal.

I returned to the scroll case area and entered the last draft tube tunnel. I found some leakage from under that gate, but it wasn't strong and the rest of the inspection was uneventful. Actually, by the time I was exiting the last tunnel, I was quite relaxed and confident, although I was getting really cold. While climbing up the ladder toward the access hatch I knew I had been tested, and I had learned a critical lesson. Because I was able to finish the job, in spite of the incident, I felt good and I felt like a real commercial deep-sea diver.

Later that evening Bill and I were talking after dinner, and I told him about my experience in the draft tube. His face grew somber as he listened carefully to my account of the incident. Then he said, "Spence, if I had known, I probably would have pulled you out of there." "I know", I answered, "and I may not have ever wanted to go back again."

We both sat silent for a few moments and Bill look directly into my eyes. The stern and serious face he held throughout my confession began to soften and a faint smile broke out. He looked down at the table and shook his head slowly. Then he raised his glass, gesturing toward me. "Here's to guts and glory," he toasted. "May we never have to sacrifice one to get the other." I joined him in the toast with an "amen." After that night there was a special bond between us, and he always looked out for me as a diver and a son.

In the three and a half years I worked for Bill Harris we did diving work on the Fort Peck Dam in Glasgow Montana, more work on the Garrison Dam, a specialized job for the U.S. Naval electronics laboratory on Pend Oreille Lake near Farragut, Idaho, and we had one very unique job on a ranch near Ephrata, Washington.

The job in Ephrata was another tunnel job, except this tunnel was vertical and extremely small—"claustrophobia small"! It involved locating a pipe that had broken off in a rancher's water well. I used scuba diving gear and was lowered 145 feet down inside a 39-inch well casing. At the bottom of the well casing I had to dive 15 feet underwater to locate the pipe and repair the system. My underwater light was nearly useless because the water was muddied with silt, so I was trying to locate the broken pipe by feel.

I felt around on the bottom and my hand located a hard, round object covered with long fuzzy material. I pulled the object close to my light and what I could make out from the distorted image caused me to freeze in place. The thought that I might be holding a severed human head made my imagination run wild.

I summoned up my courage and ascended to the surface of the water in order to make a positive identification. When I pulled the object above the water level to get a clear look at it in the light, I saw that I was holding a large, dead cat with extremely long hair. At that moment, I was very glad I was breathing clean compressed air and was wearing a mask that covered my nose.

I placed the dead cat on the seat of the platform that had lowered me into the well and removed my mouthpiece long enough to shout up the well to my topside crew to haul up the seat. I told them

I had found something and was sending it up to them. A diabolical grin crept over my face as I replaced the mouthpiece and prepared to descend to the bottom again. Just before I sank below the surface the dead cat must have reached the diving crew because I could hear cursing and muffled groans of disgust as they encountered the decaying animal.

I don't know why I would take such fiendish delight in knowing that I wasn't the only one that had to endure trauma on this dive, but there was a feeling of morbid satisfaction as I slowly sank back to the bottom of the well to complete my job. Needless to say, I wasn't too popular with my diving crew, so I promised to buy refreshments for everyone that evening if they would please pull me up out of the well. Later that evening we all had a good laugh over the incident. The memory of that dive in the well made me chuckle.

'What are you laughing at Spence?" asked King as he leaned over the side of the boat and looked down at me. "Oh," I answered, "I was just thinking about another place far away in another concrete shaft." King nodded and returned to the helm.

The large lock doors opened and King guided the *No-Name* back out into the Columbia. I looked out on the expanse of river that lay before us and realized that there were still many more miles to go. The river was huge and it seemed to go on forever! I put my mask in place, and bit down hard on my snorkel. "Let's go I shouted through the tube and struck out downriver again. I found out later that day I was actually recorded in the official fish count. I don't remember the actual count, but it went something like this. (### Chinook, ### Steelhead and one River Swimmer.)

CHAPTER 26

Portland

The next day I swam to Multnomah Falls, Oregon where I rendezvoused with a large yacht named, "The Periwinkle". The owner was Bart Woodyard, who also owned a well-known riverfront restaurant in Portland. We were his guests for the next two days. That night the crew and I bathed in luxury aboard the "Periwinkle".

In the morning, the popular host of a local Portland radio station joined us. He spent that day on the boat providing spot commentary on the swim from Multnomah Falls to Sand Island, our target for the day. Sand Island was just three miles upriver from Portland. There was a huge reception planned for our arrival in Portland the next day.

We spent another great night aboard the Periwinkle, and the next morning an obnoxious little man came aboard. He said he was the publicity coordinator for the arrival ceremony. He was abrasive and self-important, and he was extremely disturbed that at 6:30 a.m. I wasn't dressed into my gear and ready to start swimming toward the Portland staging area.

I tried to explain to him that swimming down river with a moderate pace to the landing site wouldn't take more than 30 to 40 minutes, but he wasn't convinced and was worried that we would be late. He said that if we were late, the media might not wait and that we would ruin the reception. We would also keep the Mayor of Portland, a former Miss USA, and the current Festival Queen waiting! I silently dubbed him Mr. Obnoxious.

Mr. O. kept fidgeting and checking the time as we ate our breakfast. He almost had a stroke when I said I planned to start swimming downriver at 8:15 a.m. to make the 9:00 a.m. appearance. At about 20 minutes to 8:00 a.m. he could contain his frustration no longer and became a gigantic pain, insisting that I start immediately so I wouldn't be late and gum up his publicity plans! More to get rid of him than anything else, I capitulated and told him we would start at 8:00 a.m. He wasn't completely satisfied and went off muttering to himself about something.

At 8:00 a.m., as promised, I jumped into the Columbia from the deck of the yacht and started swimming toward Portland. I tried to adjust my speed to arrive in Portland at the assigned time. With some slow floating and pacing I arrived just outside the entrance to the marina and started treading water against the current. At 10 minutes to 9:00 a.m., we noticed, Mr. O. waving at us from the entrance to the marina. My boat crew sailed over and talked with him for a few minutes, and then came back to midriver where I was marking time, wasting precious energy, and working on my weight-loss program. Mr. O. said that the dignitaries were late and we had to wait until they arrived!

At 9:00 a.m., we were given a signal to continue holding. At 9:15 we were still on hold and I figured I had swum another two or three miles going nowhere! At 9:30 a.m., still holding, I was starting to become irritated with Mr. O. and his timing! At 9:45, Mr. O. started waving his arms frantically and motioned for me to swim into the docks. When I swam around at the end of the marina jetty, I was surprised to see a very large crowd of people surrounding the docks and boat slips. I was directed around the piers to an empty boat slip where the dignitaries waited behind a huge banner welcoming me to Portland!

When I reached the end of the slip where the welcoming committee stood, I discovered that no one had thought to provide a ladder or some way for me to get up onto the dock, which was about three feet above the surface of the water. Television cameras were rolling, news people were talking into their microphones, and everyone was waiting for me to climb out of the water. Frustrated with the situation, I did an abrupt surface dive and pushed off the bottom, which was about 8 feet deep. The buoyancy of the wetsuit and the extra push off the bottom helped me propel my upper body high enough above the surface to grab the mooring rail and pull myself up onto the dock.

Once on the dock, I pulled off my fins and stood up to shake hands with the mayor, hug the former Miss USA, and get a wreath and a kiss from the Queen of the Rainmaking Festival, or something like that! We had just completed the welcoming ceremony when Mr. O. came running to inform us that Channel X had just arrived; could we stage the arrival again for them? I gave the wreath back to the festival queen, put on my fins and went back into the water. Mr. O. wanted the complete arrival, so I had to swim out into the main river again and repeat the entire arrival scenario.

I had just received my handshake, hug, wreath, and kiss, and was starting to relax when Mr. O. was back again to inform us that Channel Y had just arrived and we would have to repeat the arrival for them. He then spent the next 15 minutes fussing about the lady's clothes and makeup and trying to choreograph our welcoming act. I could see that even the welcoming committee was getting a little ticked with Mr. O. and his pushy manner. Again, I gave the wreath back to the festival queen, put on my fins and swam out into the river.

This time, Channel Y had a technical problem and Mr. O. wanted me to stay out in the main river until they were ready. About this time, the temperature of the river water near my body must have risen about 10 degrees as I became more and more steamed at Mr. O and his publicity. I made up my mind that even if the President of the United States were the next one to arrive late, that this would be my last entrance into Portland.

For the third time, I sprang up onto the dock, shook the mayor's hand, got my wreath, and more hugs and kisses from the ladies. We had just completed the third arrival sequence, when Mr. O. was back in our face wanting us to move to a new location on the dock and do it one more time. I looked directly at Mr. O. and shook my head, "No"!

I glanced passed Mr. O. and saw looks of relief on the faces of my welcoming committee. Mr. O. was visibly upset. He turned and walked to the edge of the dock and stood facing the water with his back to us. He was motioning and shouting out to some of the media that we were done. He began muttering under his breath about us all being ingrates and not appreciating what he was doing for us, or something to that effect.

I'm not sure how Mr. O. managed to lose his balance and fall off the dock. Although he claims he was pushed, I certainly didn't think any accidental bump he got from somewhere was hard enough to knock him into the water. Since I was closest to him, I reached down and grabbed his wrist as he bobbed to the surface, sputtering profanities. With the help of my brother-in-law, John, we pulled him up onto the dock and tried to act concerned as we both fought back our tears (of laughter)! Mr. O was not a happy man and wouldn't talk to any of us as he stomped off down the dock, leaving a trail of water and wet footprints.

I don't really know what the dignitaries thought of Mr. O's impromptu swim, but I could almost swear I saw the faint hint of an approving nod and caught a subtle wink from certain members of the committee. Later that evening, I received the keys to the city of

Portland. We traveled around Portland to various activities and the people of Portland were warm, wonderful, and very supportive.

The next day, we turned our focus on the final 85 miles of Columbia River between Portland and Astoria, Oregon. We anticipated that the river below Portland would be difficult because of the ocean tides, which have an effect on the river as far inland as Longview, Washington. We also expected more large boat traffic because Portland was a seaport; barges and ocean-going ships would be hauling cargo on that stretch of the river.

From Portland, I swam to St. Helens, Oregon, where I received the key to that city and some warm personal greetings from John Leonard, a close friend of our family who had worked with my dad in Lewiston. We spent the night in St. Helens as guests of the town and got back into the river very early the next morning.

Our daily mileage was getting shorter now because of the tides and some diverse river channel routing, but in spite of the slow pace and diversions due to heavy boat traffic, we still made our target for the day and reached Gobel, Oregon.

Campbell Reaches Portland Outskirts

PORTLAND (AP) — The Orofino, Idaho, man who is swimming to the ocean, reached the outskirts of Portland Monday.

Spencer Campbell, who started his swim in Idaho July 2, will travel the few remaining miles to Portland Tuesday morning. He expects to climb out of the Columbia River at a wharf restaurant at 11:30 a.m.

Campbell reached Sand Island, just east of Portland, Monday after swimming about 20 miles from Multnomah Falls.

He expects to spend Tuesday in Portland, then to plunge into the river again, hoping to reach Astoria by the weekend.

Orofino Man on Last Lap Toward Sea

July 27, 1962

LONGVIEW, Wash. (AP) — Long-distance swimmer Spencer Campbell of Orofino, Idaho, planned to swim with the tide Saturday for Astoria, at the mouth of the Columbia River.

Campbell arrived in Longview Friday night and spent the night here. Mayor Lewis Clark had breakfast with Campbell and his crew this morning and presented him a trophy from the city.

Campbell is making the 550-mile swim from Orofino via the Snake and Columbia rivers to publicize Orofino.

Campbell is scheduled to arrive in Astoria Sunday afternoon, but he said his time in covering the 50 miles will depend on how far he can get out on the ebb tides.

CHAPTER 27

~~~~~~~~~
~~~~~~~~~

Cathlamet

rom Goble, the next leg was to Longview, where the local Chamber Of Commerce planned a welcome celebration for early evening. Unfortunately, the tides turned, delaying our progress and spoiling the reception. We didn't make it to Longview until about 11:00 p.m. It was a very long, tough day of swimming, and I was so tired that I didn't have the strength to climb into the boat. I had to be helped by my brother Bill.

An officer of the Chamber of Commerce met us at the dock when we arrived and took us to the hotel where the City had arranged rooms for us. I felt bad that we couldn't get there in time for the planned celebration, but they were very understanding. Seeing how fatigued and weak I was, they knew I had tried my best! In the morning, we met the Mayor of Longview and a couple of people from the Chamber of Commerce. We had breakfast and they presented me with some gifts from the town and a huge bath towel that I was supposed to use to dry myself off at the end of the swim.

It was obvious now that we would have to adjust the swimming schedule to compensate for the tides. This meant swimming late at night and at odd times when we could make the best progress. We also knew that barring a catastrophic setback we would beat Lewis and Clark's time to Astoria. The challenge now was to see how fast we could make it!

There were three more legs to swim. The first was from Longview to Cathlamet, a very small logging town situated on the banks of the Columbia, about 60 miles downriver from Longview. The second leg was from Cathlamet to Tongue Point, just six miles upriver from our final destination in Astoria. The last leg was from Tongue Point to the city docks in Astoria, and the end of a very, long swim. A couple of exciting things happened on the last three legs. One was when we arrived in Cathlamet at about 11:00 p.m. to find that we had foiled the small town's reception, and all but a couple of people figured we were not coming and went home to bed.

Cathlamet is a logging town and most of the people had put in a hard day's work. They grew tired waiting for me to get there, but because of the tides we couldn't oblige. When we pulled into the city dock, a very inebriated two-man welcoming committee met us. They had decided to keep a vigil for us from the local tavern. When they saw us tying up the *No-Name*, they came down to the dock and announced that they were the only two left of the welcoming committee, but by God they were not going to leave until we got there! I apologized for ruining the reception and explained about the tides slowing us down and keeping us from making our planned schedule. They were not upset and said it was too bad everyone had left before we arrived.

After we secured the boat, we walked up into the town square toward the tavern, which was the only place that seemed to be open. As we reached the center of town, one of our slightly incapacitated hosts said he was going to go ring the town fire bell, and get everyone up to come and visit with us. It took some convincing to dissuade him from actually ringing the bell.

In the tavern, we met another man who seemed to be quite

sober and he tried to rustle up something for us to eat. He said that there was about forty or fifty people that got together for the welcoming, but they all left, figuring that we wouldn't be able to make it at all.

He said that one little boy about eight years old, who was confined to a wheel chair, was really disappointed because he was a big fan of the river swim. He had collected all of the press clippings and kept track of my progress every day since the swim began. He was hoping to meet me and get an autograph for his River Swim Scrapbook.

The boy's family lived about six miles north of Cathlamet on a small acreage in the woods. They brought the little boy into town for our scheduled arrival around 7:00 p.m. They waited until about 10:00 p.m. before they gave up and went home. We had about two and a half hours until the tide would turn and we could return to the river.

"Do you know anyone who could take me out to the boy's house now?" I asked the man. "I guess I could," he replied. The man, whose name I'm sorry to say I have forgotten, took King, John, Bill, and I out to the boy's home in his Jeep. During the ride, I got very cold because I was still in my wet suit. By the time we got there on the rough logging road, I was freezing.

The boy's parents were still up; they were thoroughly surprised to see us when we knocked on their door. The young boy was in bed, and his parents went in to tell him that I had come to see him. We went into his room and sat on his bed and told him stories about the river swim. All of us signed his scrapbook and we made him an official member of the swim crew.

It was around 2:15 a.m, when we got back to Cathlamet. The tide was turning and we were anxious to try to make it to Tongue Point by morning.

We were loading the *No-Name*, and preparing to go back out into the night river again, when one of our two-man welcoming committee (who was suffering from far too much celebration) staggered off the dock and disappeared under a moored boat. I saw him sinking and dove in after him. I grabbed him by his shirt and drug him back to the surface. Bill and John and two other men helped pull him back onto the dock. After that bit of excitement we left the welcoming committee standing on the landing with their soggy, sobering colleague, and pulled out into the river.

SWIMMER REACHES LONGVIEW—Marathon swimmer Spencer Campbell, 25, of Orofino, Idaho, is helped aboard his escort boat by his brother, Bill, 16, on his late arrival in Longview Friday evening.

CHAPTER **28**

~~~~~~~~~~
~~~~~~~~~~

The Last Leg

It was about 3:30 a.m., and I had settled in to a steady swimming pace next to the *No-Name*. I was almost totally submerged in the water with only the tip of my snorkel sticking out. I was trying to keep position off the bow of the boat, when my concentration was broken by a dull "thud", "thud", "thud" sound that become louder and louder. Finally, I rolled up on my side to look at King, but before I could ask him if he could hear the sound, I saw a bright red star in the sky above King's head. Just beyond the *No-Name* a few yards, faintly illuminated by her aft, post-mounted running light, I could see what looked like a moving black wall. Suddenly, it was crystal clear. We were about to be run over by a huge ocean going ship!

The red star that I saw was the port side navigation light and the "thud-thud" was the sound of the ship's huge propeller. Before I had a chance to respond, I heard John shouting and I saw King become acutely aware of the situation. I thrust myself up onto the port side of the *No-Name*. "Get away from that ship!" I shouted as I felt her huge bow wave pushing us aside! King swung our jet boat off to the left and dragged me through the water, well clear of the big freighter.

I was amazed at how quiet she was, slicing through the dark water at a pretty fair clip. I figured that the river pilot never expected a small boat to be cruising down the middle of the Columbia at that time of the morning, and obviously, the lookout didn't see us! I guess being run over by a big ocean going freighter was not one of the hazards Lewis and Clark ever worried about! I think all of us felt that this incident raked pretty high on the excitement scale. Needless to say, my boat crew regularly checked behind us for running lights for the remainder of the night.

I arrived at Tongue Point at about 5:30 a.m. It was daylight when I swam into the large naval mooring basin located there. The Basin was a Navy storage depot harboring dozens of decommissioned Second World War Liberty Ships. We moored the *No-Name* at what appeared to be the main dock.

There was no one in sight and we figured that we wouldn't see anyone until around eight o'clock, except perhaps, some Navy security personnel. I found a big coil of large diameter mooring line and used it as a cot to lie down in and grab some sleep while my crew tried to make contact with someone in Astoria.

I actually fell sound asleep in the huge coil of line and was awaken at about eight o'clock by my crew. Gordon Sinclair, from the Orofino radio station, some naval personnel, and dignitaries from Astoria had arrived. We exchanged brief greetings and I was taken to a local motel on the outskirts of Astoria for some breakfast and a couple more hours of sleep.

We talked for a while at the hotel. Before the Astoria town fathers left, I asked them if they had a publicity director who was going to coordinate my arrival into Astoria. They looked a little bewildered by my question and said, "No", that there wasn't any such person. " Thank God," I said. They were still looking a little surprised by my comments when Gordon Sinclair started chuckling and told them that he would explain our experience in Portland as they drove back into town.

The official arrival ceremony was scheduled for 2:00 p.m. in the afternoon. The plan was to take me back to Tongue Point around noon so I could prepare for the final swim from Tongue Point to the city mooring basin. I was able to catch a couple of hours of broken sleep before being taken back to the point to start the last leg of the swim. I guess the combination of fatigue and the anticipation of finally finishing the long marathon swim had me a little on edge.

When we arrived at Tongue Point, some Navy and Coast Guard officers had gathered at the dock to see us off, and I talked with them while we waited for the word to start swimming.

CHAPTER 29

Astoria and The Future

At 12:30 p.m., I slipped into the Columbia for the last leg of a long journey and a phenomenal experience! I was still very tired from the irregular swimming schedule of the last few legs, but I was exited to be within six miles of my final objective.

When I looked beyond Tongue Point to the mouth of the Columbia, and the Pacific Ocean beyond, strong feelings welled up inside of me! That sight must have brought the same thoughts and emotions to Lewis and Clark. "There it is—Thank God we've made it!'

I swam easy for the first two miles around Tongue Point, and then I opened up the pace as I passed the Coast Guard station and headed straight for the City mooring basin. I don't know how fast I was swimming, but it was very fast, and I could hear some comments about the speed from some spectators that had joined us in their boats. As I swam the last three miles more boats joined us, but kept a respectful distance under the supervision of King. I could hear the fans, and the media, shouting encouragement and cheering me on to the finish.

As we approached the Basin, I could see a great crowd of people lining the banks of the river and standing on all the nearby docks. Bill called to me, "Spence," he said. "There are hundreds of people all over the place." Actually, over a thousand people turned out to meet us when we arrived. It was an amazing show of civic pride from the wonderful people of Astoria.

With the *No-Name* and my crew next to me, I sprinted the last fifty yards into the main boat ramp at the mooring basin. As my hands touched the bottom in about three feet of water, I rolled over into a sitting position. I raised the diving mask up onto my forehead, and just sat there staring out into the great expanse of river at the mouth of the Columbia. The cheering of the crowd directly behind me on the ramp was loud, and as I pulled off my fins and rose slowly to my feet, the cheering and applause intensified into a deafening roar! I was experiencing a long moment of fulfillment and jubilation. I did it! I actually did it! I swam the entire 557 miles and beat Lewis and Clark's time by 5 days. Slowly, I got to my feet and waded ashore where reporters and dignitaries were waiting to greet me.

I was ushered to a ceremonial stage, where after being officially welcomed to the City of Astoria, Oregon, I received another ovation. The local radio station, KAST, placed a microphone in front of me and I was asked to speak. Suddenly, too many feelings tugged at my emotions. For a moment, I had to choke back some tears of happiness and relief. "What a reception," I said. "You people of Astoria are wonderful! I know that you would all like to hear about our adventures on the swim, but please excuse me for being too exhausted right now to do the stories any justice. I will say that I know what young salmon have to go through to make their initial journey to the ocean and I can guarantee you that next year, this two legged salmon won't be swimming back upstream."

I weighed 162 pounds when I left Orofino; when I reached Astoria, I weighed 140 pounds, proof that the weight loss program was effective, though I still don't recommend it. We spent two days in Astoria. There was a banquet held in my honor where I met Mark Hatfield, the Governor of the State of Oregon.

I received some nice gifts and was made an honorary citizen of the City of Astoria. We did some sight seeing at the ocean beaches and visited the Fort Clatsop Museum, where there is a historical record and artifacts from the Lewis and Clark expedition.

On the second day a truck and trailer from Hell's Canyon Excursions Inc, arrived to take King Cole and the *No-Name* back to Lewiston. In the afternoon, we said goodbye to King, who by this time after all we had been through together, felt like a brother. When they pulled the *No-Name* past us, leaving the mooring basin, I slapped a kiss on her side. She had been our special friend and my crew's floating home for 27 days!

The next day, John, Bill, and I rode back to Orofino with Gordon Sinclair. The stretches of river that I could see as we drove eastward between Portland and the Tri-Cities were full of white caps, where the relentless upriver winds lashed at the surface current. The river seemed endless, and even though I had just swam through those same areas, it seemed strangely improbable that I had really done it! As we sped down the highway, the impact of seeing those miles and miles of river made me mentally fatigued. It was if I was still out there struggling against the wind and waves.

If Horace Greeley did say that every young man should suffer an ordeal then he would have been pleased with me! Although I had successfully conquered the rivers and achieved the goal, I began to wonder where I would go from there.

Slowly, a feeling of deep disappointment came over me. The purpose of the swim was to gain some fame and make some money. I wanted the swim to save me from my financial predicament, and allow me to start making positive progress in my life. Now, my sponsors had failed me, and I didn't see any way I could get money from the swim after the fact. After all that effort it seemed like all I would get is some fleeting notoriety and 22 pounds lighter!

I was again diving into that pool of self pity when I realized that there I was allowing doubt, despair, and blame to give me excuses for failing in life. I looked out the car window at the endless miles of river again and the events of the past 27 days played over in my mind. I could still feel the agonizing pace of swimming ten and a half hours each day. After that ordeal, could I not conquer the problems of everyday life? The swim had been like a fire, meant to forge strong metal, and right then I realized that there could be no more excuses for me!

The decisions and the pathway to my future successes or failures were mine to control. I would find a way to succeed in life and accomplish my goals. In a unique way, the river represented life. While traveling its length, you could have many setbacks. Danger might be waiting around the next bend, but preparation, the will to succeed, perseverance, and the help of God will get you through. Such was my swim, and such would be my future!

THE END

&

THE BEGINNING

27 DAYS IN ROUTE.

ASTORIAN

Great Sunset Empire

Single Copies 10c

day, July 30, 1962

Distance Swimmer Gets Big Welcome to Astoria

557 MILES

27 DAYS

Swimmer Spencer Campbell of Orofino, Ida., Sunday wound up his long swim which took him through three rivers and covered 557 miles in 27 days. He was welcomed by a crowd of Astorians at the East End mooring basin. Top photo shows Campbell after he stepped from the Columbia river talking to the crowd at the basin and to listeners of radio station KAST via microphone. From left are Chuck Farmer of KAST, Campbell, City Manager William

Cunningham, Chamber of Commerce Manager Norris Johnson and Chamber President Forrest Vaughn. Lower photo taken by Astorian photographer aboard Albert Hansen's gillnet boat shows crowd gathered on pier and boat launching ramp to view arrival of swimmer, shown just before he stepped from the water on to the ramp.